Cybercrime and Cybersecurity Research

Cybercrime and Cybersecurity Research

Cybersecurity and Digital Forensics: Challenges and Future Paradigms
Abdulrahman Yarali, Randal Joyce and Faris Sahawneh
2022. ISBN: 978-1-68507-810-2 (Hardcover)
2022. ISBN: 979-8-88697-013-5 (eBook)

Global Cybercrime and Cybersecurity Laws and Regulations: Issues and Challenges in the 21st Century
Shahid M. Shahidullah, Carla D. Coates and Dorothy Kersha-Aerga
2022. ISBN: 978-1-68507-755-6 (Hardcover)
2022. ISBN: 978-1-68507-854-6 (eBook)

Cybersecurity in the Current Framework of the EU and Italian Criminal Justice Systems. A Focus on Digital Identity Theft
Clara Pettoello-Mantovani
2022. ISBN: 978-1-68507-583-5 (Hardcover)
2022. ISBN: 978-1-68507-688-7 (eBook)

Cybersecurity Risk Management: An Enterprise Risk Management Approach
Kok-Boon Oh, and Bruce Ho
2022. ISBN: 978-1-68507-428-9 (Hardcover)
2022. ISBN: 978-1-68507-505-7 (eBook)

More information about this series can be found at
https://novapublishers.com/product-category/series/microbiology-research-advances/

Kennedy Njenga
Editor

Information Systems Security in Small and Medium-Sized Enterprises

Emerging Cybersecurity Threats in Times of Turbulence

Copyright © 2022 by Nova Science Publishers, Inc.
DOI: https://doi.org/10.52305/KSVB7323

All rights reserved. No part of this book may be reproduced, stored in a retrieval system or transmitted in any form or by any means: electronic, electrostatic, magnetic, tape, mechanical photocopying, recording or otherwise without the written permission of the Publisher.

We have partnered with Copyright Clearance Center to make it easy for you to obtain permissions to reuse content from this publication. Simply navigate to this publication's page on Nova's website and locate the "Get Permission" button below the title description. This button is linked directly to the title's permission page on copyright.com. Alternatively, you can visit copyright.com and search by title, ISBN, or ISSN.

For further questions about using the service on copyright.com, please contact:
Copyright Clearance Center
Phone: +1-(978) 750-8400   Fax: +1-(978) 750-4470   E-mail: info@copyright.com.

NOTICE TO THE READER

The Publisher has taken reasonable care in the preparation of this book, but makes no expressed or implied warranty of any kind and assumes no responsibility for any errors or omissions. No liability is assumed for incidental or consequential damages in connection with or arising out of information contained in this book. The Publisher shall not be liable for any special, consequential, or exemplary damages resulting, in whole or in part, from the readers' use of, or reliance upon, this material. Any parts of this book based on government reports are so indicated and copyright is claimed for those parts to the extent applicable to compilations of such works.

Independent verification should be sought for any data, advice or recommendations contained in this book. In addition, no responsibility is assumed by the Publisher for any injury and/or damage to persons or property arising from any methods, products, instructions, ideas or otherwise contained in this publication.

This publication is designed to provide accurate and authoritative information with regard to the subject matter covered herein. It is sold with the clear understanding that the Publisher is not engaged in rendering legal or any other professional services. If legal or any other expert assistance is required, the services of a competent person should be sought. FROM A DECLARATION OF PARTICIPANTS JOINTLY ADOPTED BY A COMMITTEE OF THE AMERICAN BAR ASSOCIATION AND A COMMITTEE OF PUBLISHERS.

Additional color graphics may be available in the e-book version of this book.

Library of Congress Cataloging-in-Publication Data

ISBN: 979-8-88697-390-7

Published by Nova Science Publishers, Inc. † New York

Contents

Preface		 vii
Chapter 1	Information Systems Security in SMEs and Emerging Cybersecurity Threats	1
Chapter 2	An Overview of the Disciplines of Information Systems Security and Cybersecurity and the Role these Fields Play in SMEs	9
Chapter 3	Technology Evolution in SMEs	29
Chapter 4	Information Systems Security Behavior and Culture in SMEs	37
Chapter 5	Information Systems Security and the Role of Women Entrepreneurs in SMEs	45
Chapter 6	Novel and Emergent Information and Cybersecurity Threats Facing SMEs during Lockdowns	59
Chapter 7	Protecting Small Business Information in the Advent of Innovative Business Ideas	67
Chapter 8	The Fourth Industrial Revolution and Information Security for SMEs	75
Chapter 9	Synopsis to Information Security in SMEs and the Future of Technology	85
About the Author		91
References		93
Index		101

Preface

The title of this book is *Information Systems Security in Small and Medium-sized Enterprises: Emerging Cybersecurity Threats in Times of Turbulence.* This book is an outcome of a review of literature on the possible concern and issues Small and Medium-sized Enterprises (SMEs) would face when adopting the fourth industrial revolution (4IR) technologies. From the review of current and past literature, this book disseminates insightful ideas and developments in the field of information and cybersecurity. It is intended that these ideas will shape how SMEs now and in the immediate future address information and cybersecurity risks.

This book provides insights to information and cybersecurity scholars interested in SME information security risk management issues as SMEs increasingly adopt 4IR technologies. Information security risks such as emergent, highly sophisticated external attacks targeted at SMEs, the nature of these attacks, and the possible mitigating measures are discussed in the book.

This book is also of particular interest to information security administrators managing SME information security, who may gather additional insights on the emergent information security threats facing SMEs that are discussed in the book. A key consideration for this book is the innovative ways that SMEs have adopted 4IR technologies but, in doing so, have attracted unknown information and cybersecurity risks. The book raises awareness regarding how SMEs can remain competitive and contribute to the growth of economies globally, yet possibly harness the power of 4IR technologies while remaining secure against information and cybersecurity threats. The detailed background to cybersecurity and information security in SMEs is discussed. The chapters of this book are structured as follows:

Chapter 1 discusses SMEs' vital role in job creation and economic development through the adoption of 4IR technologies. Importantly, this chapter discusses the information and cybersecurity risks these SMEs expose themselves to when they adopt these technologies. The chapter has presented an overview of cybersecurity and information security as crucial concerns when SMEs use these technologies.

Chapter 2 introduces two overlapping and often confusing disciplines of information security and cyber security. The chapter explains the body of knowledge embedded in these two similar but distinct fields which address threats to the security of SME data, namely, information systems security and cybersecurity. The chapter addresses common confusion in these two terms partly because the discourse around these two fields often overlaps. The chapter point to advances in security threats that need to be addressed by training and awareness. A point is made for training and awareness of employees working in SMEs for the need to understand these two areas that will affect how SMEs are run.

Chapter 3 strengthens the argument that in pursuit of competitiveness in a changing global economy, SMEs have evolved and adopted technologies in innovative ways. This chapter addresses the historical development of technology in use by SMEs and the evolution of cybersecurity risks that have accompanied these technologies.

Chapter 4 discusses the prevailing information security culture and behavior that characterizes the running of SMEs. The chapter addresses the role of an insider (employee of an SME) as a security threat. A framework that SMEs could use to govern and manage cybersecurity incidents is provided in this chapter as well.

Chapter 5 discusses information systems security and the role of women entrepreneurs in SMEs. The chapter highlights women's initiatives and the advocacy of better female representation in the information security and cybersecurity profession. The role of women's entrepreneurship, the challenges women have faced, and how women have broken the barrier into cybersecurity and information security careers are discussed.

Chapter 6 discusses novel and emergent information and cybersecurity threats that faced SMEs during lockdowns instigated by the COVID-19 pandemic. The chapter discusses the surge in online activities witnessed during lockdowns, the shift to 'working from home,' and the resultant information security incidents that arose.

Chapter 7 discusses how small businesses' information may be protected in the advent of innovative business ideas. This chapter focuses specifically on new and future business innovations and ideas such as doing business in the Metaverse and how SMEs would protect their information as they adopt these technologies.

Chapter 8 examines the fourth industrial revolution (4IR) and the context in which SMEs operate and elaborates on the possible 4IR tools that include artificial intelligence, machine learning, big data, and the Internet of things that SMEs may deploy in various settings to mitigate against cybersecurity threats.

Chapter 9 provides a synopsis of the book.

In conclusion, it is envisaged that this book brings some new knowledge to readers regarding information security threats small business managers face when they adopt technology in order to remain competitive. The book endears to provide comprehensive knowledge and application of information systems security to SMEs. I want to express my sincere appreciation to the editors of Nova Science Publishers for their hard work in getting this book ready for publication. I am grateful for the publication of this book with the support of the Department of Higher Education (DHeT) of South Africa for providing funding towards this book.

Kennedy Njenga, PhD
University of Johannesburg, South Africa

Chapter 1

Information Systems Security in SMEs and Emerging Cybersecurity Threats

1.1. Introduction

At the start of Condorcet's Esquisse manuscript, published in 1795 and cited by Avery (2012, p. 6), Condorcet states that,

> "Nature has no bounds on the improvement of human facilities" and that the "intellectual and moral facilities of man are capable of continuous and steady improvement." (Avery, 2012, p. 7)

It would seem that Condorcet's early predictions have since borne fruition, with society progressively evolving to what we now refer to today as the fourth industrial revolution (Bulgurcu, Cavusoglu, & Benbasat, 2010). Clearly, in the same way that local and regional small business networks progressively improved during the early 19th century (Acs & Preston, 1997), the 21st century presents us with global business systems of production and distribution that have evolved rapidly due to advancements in technology. Businesses, including small and medium-sized enterprises can now access advanced technologies such as the Internet of things and artificial intelligence (Armenia, Angelini, Nonino, Palombi, & Schlitzer, 2021), to make them competitive (Hansen & Bøgh, 2021). Not surprisingly, we continue to witness a deep urge for steady improvements across many spheres of technology and business operations in a new globalized world characterized by advanced socio-structured systems and increased reliance on information technology (Georgiadou, Mouzakitis, & Askounis, 2021) and computer networking.

Many SMEs operate in a highly advanced, globalized, and technologically interconnected world. SMEs compete for the same markets as their larger, financially endowed big businesses. In a highly competitive business environment, SMEs must continue striving for improvement and innovation to sustain performance and competitiveness due to their essential role in a globalized economy (Markovic et al., 2021). In early 1998, the

International Labour Conference (ILC) adopted the International Labour Office's Job Creation in Small and Medium-Sized Enterprise Recommendation (No. 189) to guide job creation by SMEs (Gilovich, Medvec, & Chen, 1995). It remains to date, the only ILO Recommendation that deals explicitly with SMEs. (InternationalLabourConference, 2015). Moving forward to later years, the 104th International Labour Conference (2015) has presented solid evidence that SMEs continue to be significant job creation engines, with younger SMEs disproportionately contributing more to employment.

SMEs are essential in developing countries' economic growth (Motau & Kalema, 2016). For example, in countries such as Malaysia and Chile, the SME sector contributes more to population employment (Schaeffer & Olson, 2014; Motau & Kalema, 2016). In South Africa, SMEs create jobs 15 times more than big businesses; 90% of new jobs are created by SMEs (Leboea, 2017). The South African Department of Trade and Industry classifies business sizes according to a business's annual turnover. The National Small Business Act 102 of 1996 is the framework used in South Africa to define five South African business classes: Sector or subsector, enterprise size, number of employees, annual turnover, and gross assets excluding fixed property.

SMEs which have adopted computing technology to address business needs and to remain competitive can be identified using three categories. The first category is the 'moms and pops'; the second is the 'less than a few hundred employees with a dedicated IT staff; and the third is those that 'outsource technical assistance to third parties' (Bhattacharya, 2013). In the moms and pops category, the SME will have essential software installed on a home computer, which may also serve as a business computer. The SME will often not rely on skilled professionals for technical assistance. In the second category, the SME will often have a dedicated information system and rely on their IT staff for technical assistance. In the third category, the SME will outsource most of their technical support to third-party vendors depending on the vendor's training and reliability.

Taking note of the significant role that SMEs play in the global economy, it follows that SMEs should be protected from the emergent cybersecurity threats that accompany the use of IT in 4IR. While big businesses continue to invest heavily in protecting their information systems infrastructure from emergent cybersecurity threats such as viruses, malicious software (malware), phishing, pharming, extortion, and financial fraud, SMEs lack the necessary resources and skills to manage these threats.

Indeed, two decades back, Gupta and Hammond (2005) raised a concern that leadership style and level of concern to information security issues were contributors to how SMEs addressed threats, resulting in the delayed or incorrect implementation of information systems security measures. This concern should have been addressed in principle, but ten years later, leadership style was still considered a significant concern (Humaidi & Balakrishnan, 2015). Currently, leadership style and resource constraints in SMEs remain a barrier to SME agility and innovation (Bueechl, Haerting, Pressl, & Kaim, 2021).

1.2. A Period of Turbulence and Uncertain Times for SMEs

SMEs continue to face many challenges, but the year 2019 was unprecedented for almost all SMEs globally. A pandemic caused by the coronavirus, popularly known as COVID-19, led to the shutting down SMEs' operations globally for intermitted periods at a time. Those technologically driven SMEs that did not require a physical presence to continue operating continued to do so but quickly became targets for cybercriminals and hackers (Lallie et al., 2021).

Technology savvy SMEs moved most meetings and document transfers to virtual operations, with the close watch by cyber criminals out to carry out nefarious activities that targeted these perceived soft targets. Cybersecurity immediately became a global concern. Governments in the United States (U.S.) and the United Kingdom (U.K.) started issuing advisories. In the U.S., for instance, the Department of Homeland Security Cybersecurity and Infrastructure Security Agency published a joint advisory on how cybercriminals and advanced persistent threat groups were exploiting the current COVID-19 pandemic (Lallie et al., 2021). In the U.K., National Cyber Security Centre (NCSC) discussed issues with their U.S. counterparts on cybersecurity threats such as phishing, malware, and tools to compromise virtual meeting spaces such as Zoom (Pranggono & Arabo, 2021).

1.3. A Brief Overview of Information Systems Security

Due to rampant computer abuse by cybercriminals witnessed over the years and the accelerated abuse during intermittent lockdowns, when many SMEs are operated remotely, the security of information systems (IS) continues to be a significant concern. When SMEs started adopting computing technologies, various models were proposed on how to make these systems secure. Indeed, Information and Cybersecurity preparedness is quickly emerging as a critical area of management competency that is key to business survival, with questions being raised as to the level of responsibilities that small businesses managers should take on such competency (Chatterjee, 2019).

The idea of information and cybersecurity can be demonstrated as far back as Second World War when one of the lesser-known war heroes named Alan Turing assisted in the war efforts by turning the war to America's advantage through his brilliant code-breaking skills. He was instrumental in breaking Germany's Enigma code (Copeland, 2012). In 1943, Turing developed a code-breaking machine capable of deciphering two messages within a minute.

During the war, Germany's U-boats were sinking important supply ships to Britain, and Turing's machine broke the code that was intercepted between the U-Boats. Turing's machine enabled supply ships to avoid the U-boats and transport the supplies to Britain. The code-breaking ability advanced when Turing and other code-breakers were able to crack the code for another German machine. 'The Tunny' was used as a line of communication between Adolf Hitler and the Army High Command. The code-breaking ability provided valuable intelligence to know what the Germans were planning, thus saving millions of lives (Copeland, 2012).

In the field of information and cybersecurity, the interception by the Tunny, is known as a man-in-the-middle attack. Cybercriminals use modern advanced tools to execute man-in-the-middle attacks by intercepting communication between computers connected through the Internet. Understanding threats such as man-in-the-middle attacks led many researchers and practitioners in the early 1990s to think about developing more robust frameworks for critically understanding threats to information systems.

Baskerville (1993) observed that in the many decades after the war, advances had been made in developing information systems design methods. He pointed out that there was lagging in developing security systems and cybersecurity efforts in tandem. At a speech to the 13th National Computer Security Conference on 3rd October 1990, the then U.S. Assistant Director for National Security Affairs, Executive Office of the President, Michelle VanCleave, stated the following 'I believe I have developed that model'. She was referring to a concern raised regarding the need to develop a comprehensive model for understanding threats to information systems. The model she proposed was positioned as unique, capable of being independent of any technology, with universal application, and not constrained by differences within various organizations. By then, the security of information systems,

> "Concerned itself with the maintenance of three critical characteristics of information: confidentiality, integrity and availability," with these three attributes representing "the full spectrum of security concerns in an automated environment" (McCumber, 1991, p. 329).

Confidentiality ensures that only those users that have been allocated the proper rights and privileges to access SMEs' information are accorded the ability to do so. In order to protect the confidentiality, SMEs should use the proposed measures;

1. classify the information they have;
2. make sure that there is proper storage of any information they have;
3. develop bespoke information security policies that can protect the SMEs from external threats and attacks;
4. educate users.

Integrity addresses information that should be in its expected state, and that should be trusted. The integrity of an SME's information can be compromised when the information is exposed to any form of corruption or any form of damage, which will alter its original expected state.

Availability enables any SME user to access information without intentional or unintentional interference and obstruction to the information requested in the required time and format.

The CIA perspective coined by McCumber (1991) withstands the test of time. Current literature, accords, confidentiality, integrity, and availability, commonly known as the CIA triad as the dominating definition (Lundgren & Möller, 2019). Some scholars point out that the CIA triad was not intended as a definition and have pointed out that it,

> "Supplies goals for a secure system rather than serving as a definition supplying a demarcation between secure and insecure information (systems)." (Lundgren & Möller, 2019, p. 421)

1.3.1. A Brief Overview of Technology Evolution in SMEs

In a highly competitive global economy, SMEs need to meet global standards on technology use, quality of goods and services, as-well-as pricing (Singh, Luthra, Mangla, & Uniyal, 2019). In order to be effective job creators and contributors to industrial growth, particularly in developing countries, many SMEs have started applying information and communication technology (Gilovich et al.) to sustain growth (Singh et al., 2019). Highly advanced countries such as Germany have gone further and been leading in 4IR manufacturing (Sommer, 2015). Studies show that the application of 4IR technologies by SMEs may provide a positive direction to achieving sustainable operations and corporate social responsibilities (Kumar, Singh, & Dwivedi, 2020).

As SMEs continue to grow and use technology to remain competitive, they become critical contributors to the development of a country's economy by assisting in job creation and in reducing poverty. The global SME sector has been primarily responsible for a sizable percentage of the gross domestic product (GDP), with some developing countries in the global South, such as Chile and Brazil, accounting for 57% and 59% of GDP respectively and South Africa 36% of GDP (Leboea, 2017).

4IR technologies have helped shape how these SMEs operate and continue to contribute to GDP. 4IR technologies for SMEs vary and would include the Internet of things (IoT), additive manufacturing, cybersecurity with blockchain, augmented reality with artificial intelligence, cloud computing, big data, system integration, simulation, and autonomous robot (Kumar et al., 2020). Most of these technologies may seem futuristic and perhaps out of reach to many SMEs, with even fewer having the capacity to leverage these technologies' potential use fully. In addition, Luthra and Mangla (2018) have raised a concern that owner-managers of SMEs are not doing enough to create employee awareness regarding how these 4IR technologies can be used for ethical and sustainable operations.

1.3.2. A Brief Overview of Information Systems Security and Cybersecurity in SMEs

According to Müller, Buliga, and Voigt (2018), SMEs that innovate and apply innovative business models that may address the safe and secure use of information systems become better positioned to be competitive. Security concerns would include stolen propriety information and the external deactivation of production systems, causing a denial of vital services. SMEs, are therefore encouraged to be responsible for their data and data security across supply chain partners through reliable data transfer (Müller et al., 2018).

1.4. Conclusion

This chapter has discussed SMEs' vital role in job creation and economic development through adopting 4IR technologies. The importance of information and cybersecurity risks that SMEs expose themselves to in pursuit of economic growth was brought to the fore. An overview of how information security, as well as technology in use by SMEs, was discussed. The following are key points that the chapter presents.

Key Points

- To remain competitive, SMEs need to adapt to emergent technology that characterizes the fourth industrial revolution.
- SMEs' application of the fourth industrial revolution technologies may provide a positive direction to achieving sustainable operations.
- SMEs continue to be targets of cybersecurity threats and lack the necessary skills set or resources to mitigate against such threats.
- Adopting the CIA triad suggested in the information systems security domain may offer SMEs a full spectrum of security in an automated, connected environment.

Chapter 2

An Overview of the Disciplines of Information Systems Security and Cybersecurity and the Role these Fields Play in SMEs

2.1. Introduction

Chapter 1 has provided a broad overview of information systems security from SMEs' perspectives and presents the standpoint that SMEs need to adapt to emergent technologies to remain competitive in an ever-changing, technologically driven, globalized society.

The era of 4IR, which is visibly contemporaneous, provides SMEs with the opportunity to apply cutting-edge technologies that can transform SMEs into operationally efficient entities. However, in the drive to adopt 4IR technologies, the unintended consequence has seen SMEs simultaneously becoming exposed to innovative and cutting-edge cybersecurity risks which have evolved in tandem with 4IR technologies.

This chapter explains the body of knowledge that is embedded in two similar but distinct fields which address threats to the security of SME data, namely, information systems security and cybersecurity. The chapter addresses common confusion in these two terms partly because the discourse around these two fields often overlaps.

Dating back to old age days when human beings would hide what was then deemed sensitive information from one another, such as tribal secrets or plotting against each other, files containing such information were literally kept under lock and key. Many generations later, this present generation has witnessed the age of 4IR, which is characterized by electronic document storage, and intelligent and artificial intelligence systems, which share vast volumes of data at super-fast speeds across the globe. The need to protect such information despite advances in mode or storage still remains the same. This is more so when information is classified as sensitive. This example can be loosely addressed from the field of information systems security. Once businesses started using connected computing technologies to share information across the Internet, they started exposing themselves to computer threats such as viruses and malware. The rise of the risk of computing technologies in the age of 4IR has brought rise to a new field called cybersecurity.

The chapter starts by providing a general overview of the information systems typical in a SMEs environment and why it is necessary to protect these systems in Section 2.2. What follows is a discourse on the distinct difference between the fields of information systems security and cybersecurity, as well as the role both these fields play in SME threat management in Section 2.3. This difference is expounded. Following this, Section 2.4 provides an overview and role of information systems security in SMEs. Section 2.5 provides an overview and role of cybersecurity in SMEs.

2.2. SMEs Information Systems

Many SMEs often use information systems to address their routine operational needs; such are information processing, storage, and retrieval. SMEs are primarily concerned with addressing their customer needs in the best way possible, including getting the correct information to produce quality goods or services. In return, the SMEs become better positioned to retain these customers. SMEs also often face considerable challenges because of their business operations' voluminous data. Some of such data is valuable and provides actionable insights, and care must be taken to protect such information. Insights obtained from SME data can provide opportunities for SME growth and achieve a competitive advantage. The components of SME information systems are explained in the next section.

2.2.1. SME Transaction Processing Systems

When SMEs perform routine day-to-day operations, this result in the creation of volumes of data such as cash receipts, invoices, goods received notes, and so forth that can be captured using a transaction processing system (TPS). The TPS allows SMEs to capture data, store and retrieve such data and even process or modify such data in real-time. TPS will allow an SME owner, manager, or even employee to enter transactional information using an input system that can be a keyboard or a bar code scanner through a point-of-sale terminal. The system immediately stores this data in a database. This database can be queried, i.e., sending a request to the database system to access specific data to retrieve it and manipulate it for decision-making. This process is known as the data-driven decision-making process.

2.2.2. SME Management Information Systems

Managers who run SMEs may use a management information system (MIS) to obtain data captured by TPS in the form of current or historical data. This data can provide actionable insight created by MIS-generated visual presentations such as summary reports and charts from sales operations, useful for strategic, tactical, and operational decisions. For example, an SME manager can use a pie chart to illustrate how sales volumes per unit, per sales employee, or market are performing. Patterns from trend analysis can then inform an SME manager of the proper steps to take regarding sales. SMEs can use MIS also to carry out scenario analysis and 'what-if' to determine the effect of a lowering or an increase in a product's price.

2.2.3. SME Decision Support Systems

Managers and owners of SMEs may use decision-support systems (DSS) for data-driven decision-making through requested or ad hoc reporting requirements. For instance, managers may use DSS to generate reports that can support the present or future planning of SME sales or inventory operations and solve operational inventory problems, discounts, or commission calculations. DSS will generate answers in the form of reports to the queries the manager presents, and these solutions can be evaluated before final decisions are implemented. A DSS has a graphical user interface dashboard that visually presents these reports. An SME owner or manager can select these visual graphs to show a key performance indicator of a measure and how to move towards meeting set goals.

2.2.4. SME Executive Support Systems

Managers running SMEs can use an organizational support system to assist in identifying significant trends and patterns that SME data generates (Bueechl, Haerting, Pressl, & Kaim, 2021). These systems often serve the SMEs' long-term strategic planning and decision-making that is ordinarily non-routine. An ESS has a GUI interface that a manager can click on that specifies search criteria. The search criteria could be predefined reports and graphs sourced from SME operational data. These reports provide essential briefs to the manager regarding the strategic market, industry, and consumer trends in SME contexts. There are helpful software tools embedded in ESS systems that offer advanced analytical support for predicting projections and outcomes. These tools can also predict SME performance and statistical analysis using existing data SME data.

2.3. Information Systems Security and Cybersecurity

Information systems security and cybersecurity are two distinct fields of scientific inquiry that consider the security of SMEs' information and information systems. These two fields address the need for SMEs to protect and safeguard information from different vantage points. However, when it comes to threats to information from computerized digital environments, commonly referred to as 'cyberspace,' it is the field of cybersecurity that takes sizable prominence. Paulsen and Toth (2016) consider information security broadly outside the cyberspace realm to that of information systems protection from unsanctioned access, unsanctioned use, and as-well-as unsanctioned disclosure. They explain that information must be protected from any disruption, modification, and, importantly, destruction.

As explained by a diverse range of literature, the primary aim of information security is to provide confidentiality, integrity, and availability, commonly referred to as the CIA. The approach to information is closely related to but can be contrasted with cybersecurity which addresses the specific need to protect information stored in any electronic device. The discipline of cybersecurity formally considers how information held in electronic devices such as laptops, personal computers, mobile phones, web cameras, printers any other devices capable of storing information may be protected. Concerns for the protection of information extend to how information is communicated through network communication systems. Cybersecurity and information security become more pressing when SMEs use more and more information across the entire line of businesses and as the information becomes digitized and digitally stored, and as more complex processing of such information becomes critical to the survival of SMEs.

It is perhaps Rashid, Noor, and Altmann (2021) who have attempted to provide a discourse on these two fields in a single piece of work. They have addressed the notion of cybersecurity information sharing as a preserve for furthering awareness into both these fields and considered a promising approach to not only addressing cybersecurity threats but proactively dealing with threats before these occur. They point to information sharing as a practical approach to confronting different cybersecurity scenarios such as cybercrimes, cyberwarfare, and hacktivism. They advocate that by SMEs and other larger businesses having,

> "Accurate information, at the right time, these businesses will be better positioned to keep themselves up to date in emergent cybersecurity issues. This will, in turn, empower SME business owners with the ability to reduce cybersecurity risks, deter attackers, and enhance resilience." (Rashid et al., 2021, p. 436)

2.3.1. Approaches to Implementing Information Security in SMEs

Implementing information security programs for SMEs may differ from larger businesses. For large businesses, the implementation may follow two distinct approaches. The first approach is known as the *bottom-up approach*. This approach utilizes the skill sets and expertise of administrators who work with information systems routinely. These information systems experts are often knowledgeable regarding the security challenges they face and will most often understand the emerging threats to business systems. They will then suggest control and security features for secure business information systems.

The second approach is known as the *top-down approach*. This approach offers big businesses higher chances of implementing better security control measures because security measures are designed and supported by top and upper-level managers. Because of the strong support from upper management levels, dedicated funding, and clear planning, the implementation of information security measures is clear.

For SMEs, these two approaches may not be applicable because of the size and the skill sets of owners and managers. SMEs are relatively small to incorporate either the top-down or the bottom-up approach since the day-to-day management and running of the business is done by one or very few people. Most SMEs' and owners lack the technical skills to offer sustainable information security solutions without industry guidance. Most will therefore rely on outsiders to implement security measures. Unlike big businesses, which in most instances are required by law to report on information security incidents and breaches, SMEs are not required to report incidents. Therefore, SMEs take a lax approach to implement security measures simply to survive adverse incidents rather than keeping them continually protected. SMEs will also lack good risk management attitudes towards information security. Many practitioners point out that risk management would benefit SMEs because of the relatively small size of business and the low costs involved with understanding how to carry out their bespoke risk management and assessment activities.

2.3.2. Common Information Security Threats to SMEs Information Systems

The use of information systems across SME operations makes these systems susceptible to threats that can compromise the confidentiality, integrity, and availability of information. While many of these common threats signify a clear and present risk to SMEs, people, information, and systems, they can be managed if owners and managers make concerted efforts to understand the nature and sources of these threats. SMEs are advised to prioritize the threats each face depending on the unique operating environment each SME is in. These threats are discussed in the sections that follow.

- *Forces of nature:* At times referred to as "acts of God,' these forces can present one of the most dangerous threats to people, information assets, and technology systems of an SME. These forces would constitute unplanned natural disasters such as a fire, a flood, or an earthquake, which can cause physical damage to SME computing hardware. Natural disasters can also include pandemics such as the COVID-19 pandemic, which resulted in the shutting down of many SMEs, some of which never recovered and closed their businesses permanently.
- *Trespass:* At times, also called espionage, trespass can fall under the broad category of unauthorized information breaches to the confidentiality of information. Attackers may use different methods to obtain unauthorized access, such as stealthily manipulating a maze of control restrictions to find information. This activity is called hacking, and the perpetrators are known as hackers. Hackers may possess a variety of technical skills and understanding of

programming languages, network protocols, and operating systems to enable them to accomplish unauthorized access. Because of their extreme talent, they can constitute a significant threat to SMEs because they can gain access to SMEs' information systems and increase their control of the information systems through obtaining administrative rights and privileges. This process is known as privilege escalation.

Hackers vary depending on the tasks at hand, the skill sets, and their goals or missions. In the 1970s, some hackers called phreakers specifically focused on making free calls from public payphones. Currently, the rise in copyright abuse and the bypassing of passwords and decryption is carried out by a cracker. Both hacker and cracker represent activities that have criminal intent because most use password cracking to attempt to guess or reverse calculate a password. Indeed, many hackers have successfully cracked passwords using techniques such as brute force attacks that use software tools to try possible combinations of passwords within a short time. SMEs can protect themselves from hacking and cracking when they implement manufacturer-recommended security safeguards and continually update manufacturer software to meet the latest security standards. This process is known as patching.

- *Human failure:* In the information security domain, people have always been perceived as the weak link to the security of the systems they use. This can be attributed to human failure. People as a weak link to information security will compromise the security of systems unintentionally or by mistakes made. Poor training, inexperience, and making incorrect assumptions are leading causes of human failure in safeguarding the security of systems. Human failure can inflict severe damage to systems security.

Social engineering is an attacker's activity that takes advantage of human failure. A social engineer will exploit human weakness by falsely representing herself/himself as a genuine helper of a technical problem, only for the victim to realize that the real intention was for the person to gain access to systems illegally. Unauthorized access to systems can also be through encouraging users of SME systems to click on links known to spread dangerous viruses and malware. These links are spread by sending perceived harmless emails with dangerous links as part of a message. People will click on these links because they seem to originate from trusted sources. This technique is known as a phishing attack and will target unsuspecting and inexperienced users, many of whom are in SMEs.

- *Information Extortion:* At the time of writing this book, the credit reporting agency TransUnion South Africa has just been reported in the headline news as being a victim of a ransomware attack with a hacking group called N4aughtysecTU, which claims to be in Brazil, demanding $15million (R 225 million) ransom for over four terabytes of compromised data.

Like other ransomware attacks, the hacking group claimed that it had 54 million South Africans' credit scores, banking details, and ID numbers, threatening to release this data. Although this reported incident did not seem to be encryption, ransomware would mean data is encrypted on a user drive, and payment is needed for decrypting this data. Encryption ransomware is the worst form of attack and is difficult to recover if data has not been backed up. The Southern African Fraud Prevention Service (SAFPS) reported that every company that holds personal information is a potential target after the attack. In a separate incident, the Department of Justice in South Africa also announced that it too had been a victim of a cybercrime.

- *Sabotage:* In this category of threat, the victim's computer information systems are subjected to deliberate vandalism in order to destroy an asset or damage the image and reputation of the victim. There is a notable rise in online vandalism carried out by hacktivists. Also on the rise is cyberterrorism, which is sinister acts of destroying or defacing web pages.
- *Software:* deliberate software attacks occur when software developed to carry out an attack is designed and deployed. This malicious software called malware may include viruses and worms primarily designed to cause harm to information systems. Some worms could be advanced, such as the polymorphic worms, from the word's 'poly', meaning many, and 'morph' or change. These polymorphic worms attack as many as six known vectors to exploit vulnerabilities in information systems commonly used. Worms can replicate until they completely fill all available information systems resources such as hard drives, memory, and network bandwidth. Other software-based communication attacks can come in the form

of sniffers that can intercept packets of data traversing through the Internet. While some sniffers may be used for legitimate purposes by network specialists to monitor traffic, it has been shown that those with malicious intent have used sniffers to steal information. Sniffers can be extremely dangerous since they are virtually impossible to detect and can be found on any network.

- *Hardware:* the expected threat to hardware is an attack that can lead to hardware failure. A hardware failure attack is possible when a known flaw in hardware is exploited. Flaws in hardware may cause the system to perform sub-optimally, such as the known Intel Pentium II chip that had a defect resulting in a calculation error resulting in a chip recall costing $ 475 million.
- *Theft:* The theft of data and information will not only diminish the value but also damage a target company's reputation. Copying files without any SME knowing constitutes theft and is more difficult to control as this form of theft is electronic. As many SMEs increasingly use mobile technology such as smartphones and tablets, the greater the chances of electronic theft happening.

2.4. Overview and Role of Information Systems Security in SMEs

In 1943, International Business Machines (IBM) developed the first electronic computing machine, the 'vacuum tube multiplier'. The world was then introduced to the 1944 automatic sequence-controlled calculator, or the 'Mark 1' developed by Harvard alongside IBM (Phelps, 1980). Mark 1 was the first progenitor of what is currently known as the modern personal computer (PC). The 1950s and 1960s saw the invention of many core technologies that allowed PCs to be used by businesses. With the advent of ICTs and global PC networks growing, a worldwide integration of business processes and value chains became established, and businesses became dependent on PCs for core business processes.

Studies showed that with increased ICT use, there was a corresponding growth in PC security abuse (Kankanhalli, Teo, Tan, & Wei, 2003). Of concern in the 1990s was that the growth in PC security threats did not translate to efforts to make information systems security as expected. By the early 2000s, a global information security survey on midsized and big organizations showed that less than 50% of the Chief Information Officers (CIOs) said that they had implemented IT security training and awareness programs, with most not having such programs. Kankanhalli et al. (2003) reported a survey by the Computer Security Institute in 2002, which showed that 90% of respondents had detected security breaches, yet worrisome was that this was not enough to foster a more assertive concern for information systems security. A plausible explanation for common management concerns, as elucidated by (Straub Jr, 1990), was that management would make deliberate decisions to invest little in information systems security because they thought the risk of information security abuse was low. A second explanation that (Straub Jr, 1990) provides is that they were skeptical about the effectiveness because it was hard to evaluate benefits by then. Finally, management lacked knowledge about the possible range of controls available to reduce information systems security abuses.

Present information systems security concerns in the era of 4IR can be considered from 2 dimensions: the dimension of personalization and self-organization. The personalization dimension considers access to private and personal information from multiple information systems that manage information sourced from connected devices such as IoT. The self-organization dimension requires that management accept that communication of devices without human involvement or machine-to-machine (M2M) is automated, posing a challenge in managing secure information exchange (Din, Jambari, Yusof, & Yahaya, 2020).

Information systems security has not been considered a standalone activity but one founded on a well-developed security strategy balanced with and supporting business strategy (Barton, Tejay, Lane, & Terrell, 2016). Many SMEs usually have to navigate and overcome the often-challenging terrain of information systems security because of how these businesses operate in contrast to big businesses. The distinct nature of SMEs makes it challenging to apply information systems security approaches tailored for big businesses, and as a result, many SMEs experience information systems security failures. Studies show that SMEs are partly to blame for these failures because many seek to defend their small size to justify complacency. SMEs play a crucial role in the economy, gathering much valuable information in the process. SMEs will lack the necessary resources to store, process, or protect such information. This shortcoming comes at the expense of losing customer trust. The literature identifies four crucial factors that may enable SMEs to implement a successful information security management strategy (Ključnikov, Mura, & Sklenár, 2019). These four include;

1. Business activities compliance with information systems security policies;
2. Support of business owners;
3. Security controls; and
4. Organizational awareness.

2.4.1. Information and Cybersecurity Terminologies Relevant to SMEs

There are terminologies that the book uses that SMEs need to familiarize themselves with, which are covered in the various chapters. Some of the standard terms are as follows.

- *Access Control:* This is where an SME can prevent unauthorized manipulation and modification of SME data and information by instituting credential-based or user-based controls.
- *SME Assets:* These are the SMEs' resources that should be protected. SME assets typically include the SMEs computers (hardware and software) as tangible and intangible resources.
- *Cyber Attack:* This is the deliberate or accidental action targeted at an SME's assets that can cause damage or compromise SME information, for instance, from hackers, viruses, and malicious software (malware).
- *Information Security Posture:* This is the entire set of controls and safeguards placed by an SME that includes educating users, developing policies, and investing in security tools to protect SME assets.
- *Controls:* This is where an SME can instate measures and mechanisms, guidelines, and bespoke policies to prevent cyber-attacks on SME assets and reduce chances of risk while improving the SME information security posture.
- *Exploit:* This is where an illegal cyber-attack occurs because of a SMEs compromised or weak controls using existing software tools or custom-made tools for a specific SME.
- *Exposure:* This is where an SME's weak controls for protecting SME assets are known or made public by an attacker making an exploit successful.

- *Threats:* These are events targeted at an SME that potentially affect SME operations and SME assets adversely.
- *Vulnerabilities:* These are potential weaknesses in an SME asset or its controls, heightening the exposure of the SME asset to cyber-attacks.

2.5. Measures to Information Security and Cybersecurity in SMEs

SMEs have been shown to be at a far greater risk of experiencing a cyber-attack when compared to big businesses. More cybersecurity attacks happen to SMEs because many owner-manager will disregard or be less sensitive to the value of information or information systems these SMEs own. Most cyberattacks will target this information by taking advantage of the ill-prepared owner-managers, who may mistakenly believe that they are secure. Some of the challenges that SMEs face are the lack of policies that address the use of the cyber-space, how personal emails are to be used, and how to govern technology.

In light of the many challenges that have emerged as a result of SMEs adopting digitalization in their work processes, SMEs must apply information security and cybersecurity in conjunction, taking cognizance of the diversity of security measures available by both disciplines when applying these to localized SME contexts. SMEs that develop robust policies for information security and cybersecurity will do better than those that do not. Adopting information security and cybersecurity measures is often influenced by the tradeoff between the costs and benefits, and often these tradeoffs are mediated by attitude (Bulgurcu, Cavusoglu, & Benbasat, 2010). Some information security and cybersecurity measures, as suggested by Paulsen and Toth (2016), are shown in Table 1. Importantly, when SMEs apply these measures in wholesome to localized contexts, these measures may serve as a better defense against a wide range of threats to the SMEs. Threats to SMEs can emanate from outside of these organizations and, more recently, as studies have shown, from the inside of SMEs. Some of these measures are explained below in Table 1.

Table 1. SMEs security related measures

Measures	Explanation	Degree of importance
Cybersecurity	SMEs must apply cybersecurity measures such as being proactive in identifying potential threats and incidents to information held in electronic devices, allocating a reasonable budget to protect these devices, and learning from previous incidents.	Critical
Privacy	SMEs are mandated to protect information these collect in the ordinary process of transacting businesses. As such it is necessary for SMEs to institute sound privacy policies, and understand what needs protecting and why such protection is necessary. A balanced approach needs to be applied when determining the measure of protection against threat determination given that SMEs face constrained budgets.	Critical
Physical security	SMEs can protect physical devices such as locking these up with better locking systems, incorporating the use of a surveillance camera and have a focused training to those who work in SMEs regarding physical security measures such as not forgetting to lock assets, not allowing the presence of unauthorized persons into the SMEs premises.	Moderate to Critical
Contingency Planning and Disaster recovery	SMEs must formalize plans for business recovery in the event of an external attack. It is recommended that active continuous drills be conducted for proper employee training on proper response measures.	Critical
Operational Security	SMEs must address operational security (OPSEC) through preventing sensitive information from authorized use by unauthorized people. SMEs must be sensitive by viewing operations from the perspective of those who may have nefarious intentions towards these businesses.	Moderate to Critical
Personal security	SMEs should provide adequate measures to protect those working within its precincts by deterring, delaying, and importantly providing early warning before possible crime, or injury occurs. A proper response plan must be in place when a crime occurs and where necessary if such warning occurs, to assistance summoned.	Critical

While the above measures are not conclusive, SMEs will fare better when the above-listed measures are adopted. As Paulsen & Toth (2016) suggests, not following these measures could be detrimental to SMEs' systems, networks, and employees and may consequently negatively impact the SMEs' customers and stakeholders. SMEs should therefore contextualize these measures to their localized circumstances. It is vitally important that each small business understand and manage the risk to information, systems, and networks that support their business.

2.5.1. SME Attitude Towards Information and Cybersecurity Measures

Studies have shown that the SME owner-manager attitude towards information and cybersecurity measures is likely influenced by the level of education and technical know-how, the size of the SME, the types of activities the SME does, and importantly, the volumes of information generated by the SME. SMEs that are proactive, with owner-managers spending more person-hours expended information and cybersecurity measures, the better the information security effectiveness (Straub & Welke, 1998). Sadly, to date, many owner-managers are still not comfortable with expending this much effort. Ignoring IS security and cybersecurity threats can be detrimental, as is often the case with SME owner-managers who sometimes are overly confident in their preparedness and defense capabilities. A study on SMEs showed that 95% of IT leaders surveyed believed they had an above-average security posture (Benz & Chatterjee, 2020).

2.5.2. SME Business Risk for Not Expending Security Measures

Business risk reduction considers the steps SMEs can take in preventing data breaches and mitigating against threats posed by external attacks such as hackers and viruses (Lloyd, 2020). Effective risk mitigation strategies may enhance SME business agility and *"personalizing product offering that deliver market opportunity and business growth"* (Lloyd, 2020, p. 15). According to Randall and Allen (2021), the business risk caused by the cybersecurity threats landscape has been evolving (Georgiadou, Mouzakitis, & Askounis, 2021). The changing cybersecurity threats landscape has made it difficult for SMEs to keep up-to-date with cybersecurity control and protection measures such as patching vulnerable software and segmenting computer networks. Lloyd (2020) points out that defending SMEs against cybercrime and any other cybersecurity threat can deliver genuine benefits and may result in increased value. For example, as many as 55% of U.K. businesses faced cyber-attacks in 2019, a leap from 40% from the previous year (Lloyd, 2020). By their small size, many SMEs are considered soft targets. SMEs have attempted to be proactive in managing cybersecurity threats. Lloyd (2020) reports that during 2019, 62% of U.K. SMEs took action to identify cybersecurity risks, such as regular checks, conducting a cybersecurity risk assessment, conducting an internal audit, and, importantly, conducting an external audit. Noteworthy, however, is that only 15% of SMEs in the U.K. had a formal cyber incident management process.

SMEs that fail to adopt information and cybersecurity measures often encounter business risks. The business risk may be exemplified in the form of cybersecurity threats and the likelihood of these threats impacting adversely on the SMEs. Owner-managers of these SMEs often make daily risk-based decisions with minimal advice from professional consultants compared to larger businesses. The decision regarding whether or not to spend on anti-virus or anti-malware software, whether to install surveillance cameras and how much to invest in more secure devices can be daunting for an SME owner-manager. When the owner-managers understand the security needs of the SME, then more focused effort and direction can be expended.

It should be noted that business risk from cybersecurity threats may not be fully eliminated, but the risks can be transferred (by insurance) or minimized depending on the level of risk assessment. There are possibly times the owner-manager will have to make a reasonable judgment when trying to understand the impact the threats may have on the SMEs and how to mitigate against these. It is for such reason that SME owner-manager make use of all resources, tools, and information sharing with others for a better security posture of SMEs. Table 2 below shows an inventory of tasks and activities that can be performed by the owner-manager of the SME towards risk mitigation efforts.

Table 2. Inventory of Tasks

Risk Mitigation efforts by Owner-mangers
Identify the nature any type of information stored in the SME systems.
Determine the value of information stored in the SME systems.
Develop an inventory of information and physical assets and allocate a risk measure of these assets.
Use the risk measure to determine risk mitigation efforts.

2.5.3. Impact of Cybersecurity Risk to SMEs

Many SMEs will face constrained personnel and financial resources investing in cybersecurity risk mitigation strategies, making them soft targets to cybercriminals and others with nefarious intentions against the SMEs. SMEs may not be aware that they may hold valuable information or can be used as launch pads for attacks on larger businesses. Therefore, SMEs must understand the impact these risks can have on SMEs. These risks can be outlined as follows:

- The level of damage or loss caused to SME information and systems;
- The fines and penalties imposed by regulators for failure to comply with regulations;
- The decreased levels of business productivity and business income caused by cybersecurity events;
- The adverse business reputation that may occur as a result of a cybersecurity attack;
- The loss of trust and business credibility arising from a cybersecurity attack.

2.6. Information and Cybersecurity Controls Frameworks for SMEs

Though the impact of cybersecurity threats may pose a considerable risk to SMEs, many owner-managers acknowledge that by applying safeguards and controls, SME assets can be better managed. It is therefore crucial for SME owner-managers to understand the nature of cybersecurity attacks to design bespoke safeguards and controls suitable for their localized SME needs. To help owner-managers understand the proper safeguards and contrails that could be implemented, Benz and Chatterjee (2020, p. 532) have suggested that the following questions be asked;

- "Where is our company exposed to serious cybersecurity risks?"
- "What is an acceptable level of risk?"
- "How do we compare with others in our industry?"
- "What can we do to improve in areas where we are sub-standard?"

These questions are pertinent when owner-managers need to place proper controls but find that they are constrained by expertise and skills in adequately using technology. According to Nazareth and Choi (2015), attempts by SME owner-managers to effect proper cybersecurity safeguards and controls must develop a robust cybersecurity framework that must address the ever-changing and dynamic aspects of security threats. For many SMEs, developing a robust cybersecurity framework can be daunting.

Table 3. Information and Cybersecurity Issues for SMEs Use

NIST CSF Functions	How SMEs can effect controls for these functions
Identify	This function is recommended to SMEs when there is need to identify employees and others who have been given proper access to information and control how this access is given. SMEs can perhaps carry out background checks before access is granted and may require that those granted access are allocated accounts which are monitored. SMEs can create policies and procedures anchored on this function.
Protect	This function is recommended to SMEs when there is an identified need to limit employee access to SME information. Protection can be carried out at systems level where access is restricted. Protection can also apply to physical assets owned by SMEs such as Personal computers and monitors, mobile phones, servers, projectors etc. Tasks such as surge protector installations, running anti-virus and antimalware scans frequently, patching operating systems frequently, filtering emails, employee training and installing firewalls can enhance protection measures.
Detect	This function is recommended to SMEs when there is need to inspect whether there has been a breach or attack on the SME systems or when it is suspected that information may have been compromised. SMEs are also advised to create, maintain and monitor logs of any intrusion or breach to systems. Implementing real-time 36 intrusion detection and prevention systems (IDPS) can enhance detection measures.
Respond	This function is recommended to SMEs when there is need to address a cybersecurity incident and the proper way to do so. SMEs are encouraged to develop a plan for any potential cybersecurity threats or any disaster that may befall the SME such as novel information and cybersecurity incidents.
Recover	This function is recommended to SMEs when there is need to recover operations in the actual even of a cyberattack or any disaster that may befall the SME. SMEs are encouraged to create and maintain full backups of important information and periodically test the efficacy of these backups.

To simplify this process, the National Institute of Standards and Technology (NIST), a non-regulatory agency of the United States Department of Commerce, has created and released a cybersecurity framework (CSF) that is voluntary to follow by SMEs. The NIST CSF has gone a long way toward assisting SMEs with the proper way to prevent, detect and respond to many cyber-attacks. Some SMEs have mentioned that they feel pressured to associate with these standards and portray this to the public (Lloyd, 2020).

The NIST CSF is seen as a popular security framework that could afford SMEs' best practices while maintaining regulatory compliance. As explained by Ncubukezi, Mwansa, & Rocaries, (2020), the framework considers five concurrent and continuous functions addressing the various steps SMEs can follow, including:

- Identify
- Protect
- Detect
- Respond
- Recover

Each of these functions is explained in Table 3.

2.6.1. Useful Control Habits to Enhance Cybersecurity Awareness

Besides the NIST CSF that SMEs could adopt, there are more general behavioral recommendations that are best practices that can be applied with minimal difficulty to assist SMEs in maintaining a sound and effective cybersecurity posture. Cyber threats and attacks can be managed and even prevented when SMEs practice standard safeguards habits. Table 4 presents some of these common but valuable habits.

2.6.2. Cyber-Insurance as a Control Tool for SMEs Cybersecurity Risk

There has been an emerging need for SMEs to consider cyber insurance that could protect against cyber-attacks. Looking at the cybersecurity threat landscape that many SMEs face, cyber-insurance should now be regarded as a highly desirable option supporting SMEs' overall business strategy. There is documented evidence that SMEs that face nefarious cyber-attacks on their systems will, more often than not, also face business disruption and, at times, loss of revenues. Cyber-insurance may protect SMEs against adverse disruptions by ensuring SMEs apply best practices and fit-for-purpose security.

Table 4. Useful control habits

Useful control habits	SME consideration
Be keen on who has access to information and SME assets at all times.	Concerns have been raised that SMEs are unaware of the operating environment.
Sensitize employees and raise awareness on E-Mail risks such as phishing attacks.	Studies show that sensitized employees are less likely to be a security threat to SMEs than those who are not.
Institute 'bring your own device' (BYOD) policies that clearly delineates the use of personal (untrusted devices such as smart phones) and business devices so that abuse of internet resources like bandwidth and data is restricted.	In the advent of Mobile devices proliferating in the SME environment, managers need to manage and control these devices.
Limit the use of cyber surfing (and more commonly cyber loafing) and the ability for employees to visit unnecessary and unproductive websites and importantly the care needed in determining the kind of software to be downloaded using business data on business devices. Be careful downloading software. Advocate for employees to only visit trusted websites and not click on links to unknown sites.	A lot of time and resources have been wasted intentionally and unintentionally in unproductive Internet usage with a fraction of this time on activities that pose a security risk. Internet access should be monitored.
Encourage the use strong passwords, preferably with alpha-numeric characters and special characters and the mixed use of upper and lower cases and minimum password defaults.	Untrained employees will recycle passwords if the opportunity arises.

The current debate by cybersecurity practitioners has been divided on whether or not to pay insurance claims from cyber incidents such as ransomware attacks. This situation is akin to many global governments' standard policy of not negotiating with a terrorist, just in case these government entities fuel terrorism. The temptation for more exacerbated attacks grows for claims to be settled from ransomware attacks. Some would argue that SMEs still need to take a proactive stance on cyber-attack prevention while reducing security incident risk exposure by taking insurance.

The state of cyber insurance is currently in its infancy. Firstly, the insurance sector needs the necessary data and metrics to base predictive models of probability, and it has been suggested that are their initial stages of maturity. Insurance companies are equally considered as targets themselves, exacerbating the already existing business risk.

A lack of awareness on how to comply with cybersecurity laws such as the United Kingdom's, Data Protection Act (UKDPA) and the European Union's General Data Protection Regulation (GDPR), as well as the South Africa's Electronic Communications and Transactions (ECT) Act is manifested across many SMEs. Insurance documents may be completed as a ticking exercise to determine policy and premium with little regard for depth and knowledge in the market. Indeed, cases are starting to occur where claims are not being settled due to ambiguities between both the insurer and the insured. Indeed, the insurance may not fully appropriate a comprehensive understanding of good cybersecurity practices, compounding the problem.

2.7. Conclusion

This chapter has introduced two overlapping and often confusing disciplines of information security and cybersecurity and addresses common confusion in these two terms. The chapter addressed the need for training and awareness of employees working in SMEs regarding information and cyber security. The following are key points that the chapter presents.

Key Points

- There are two distinct but similar disciplines for protecting SMEs from threats from using technology. These are information security and cybersecurity.
- SMEs are soft targets to information and cybersecurity threats because of reduced financial and technical investments compared to big organizations.
- SMEs can be proactive and take measures to protect themselves by applying measures for protection that can be benchmarked against best practices.
- SMEs' owner-managers attitudes influenced by the level of education and technical know-how can adversely influence measures taken to protect SMEs' assets from information and cybersecurity threats.

Chapter 3

Technology Evolution in SMEs

3.1. Introduction

The era of 4IR that is visibly contemporaneous provides SMEs with the opportunity to apply innovative technologies. 4IR technologies can potentially transform SMEs into operationally efficient entities. However, in the drive to adopt 4IR technologies, the unintended consequence has been that SMEs have been simultaneously exposed to innovative and innovative cybersecurity risks, which have evolved in tandem with 4IR technologies. This chapter explains the historical development of technologies used in businesses to the present day 4IR technologies and points to why the drive to push SMEs to adopt 4IR innovative technologies is inevitable.

The chapter starts by examining the historical development of various technologies used by SMEs in Section 3.2. Following this, Section 3.3 examines the early days of technology use in SMEs and how technology has evolved. Section 3.3 provides a discourse on cybersecurity threats and how these have evolved in tandem with technological developments. It shows how cybersecurity threats are considered novel, orchestrated, multistage and evasive. The concluding Section 3.4 addresses how evolving cybersecurity threats have impacted IS governance which has also evolved.

3.2. The Historical Development of Technology in SMEs

ICT innovation has radically transformed the way businesses operate as well as how society presently interacts with both big and small businesses. In the 4IR era, society is presently witnessing a digital (r)evolution that is yet to be fully comprehended nor to predict its societal impact. The last century presented us with the industrial revolution that ponded up many business opportunities. Before the invention of computers, many businesses operated without a centralized way of communicating with each other. Most were not efficient in the slow communication methods such as ordinary mail that used inefficient postal systems. Most people working in these businesses were required to be physically present and hardly carried out any collaborative efforts.

3.2.1. Early Days of Technology Use in SMEs

In the early days when SMEs started using technology, these businesses were not exposed to many developments that we now take for granted. Elements such as electronic file sharing through email that allowed instantaneous communication was unheard of. As technology became complex and through rapid evolution, it started changing the modes and functions of work. Businesses started realizing that technology could be seen as "things–in–use" and neutral mediators to many processes. Business owners could now tailor the numerous technologies to their needs as technology started becoming neutral mediators of business operations, SMEs, and their lives, actions, experiences, perceptions, and existence change. Technology was better suited to co-shape "things–they–use."

3.2.2. Major Evolution of Technology Use in SMEs

As SMEs matured in the use of computing technology and started operating in the cyber-physical environment, SMEs started using IT to communicate, collect information, and make real-time decisions. The deployment of modern communication networks such as fourth-generation (4G) and fifth-generation (5G) mobile network capabilities has leveraged SMEs' efficiency. SMEs can now connect any device within its asset configuration, such as phones, tablets, laptops, printers, and web-based cameras (webcams) across the internet at unparalleled speeds.

3.3. Information Systems Security and Cybersecurity Threats Evolution in SMEs

The evolution of information and communication technologies can be summarized as follows: The first generation of ICT presented SMEs with technologies such as mobile computing devices that could now communicate across wireless channels. Communication is traditionally known as first generation (1G) computing in the early 1979 to mid-1980s. Following the evolution, the second generation (2G) computing technology applied the global system for mobile communications (GSM), which addresses privacy and security issues of 1G communication by encrypting communication between devices across cellular networks. 2G was designed to increase efficiency in the radio frequency spectrum, enabling more communication devices. This period also introduced the short 43 message service (SMS) technologies, where users in SMEs could now send simple short text messages to each other. In the third generation (3G) technology phase during the mid-2001, SMEs witnessed the introduction of Internet Protocol-based communication, which enabled faster text data transmission across the Internet, and the era of the mobile workforce was ushered in. (Lallie et al.)

Many SMEs currently use the fourth generation (4G) technology which provides IP telephony technology and advanced video conferencing capabilities. SMEs have started venturing into the fifth generation (5G) space developed in 2019 and planned to succeed in 4G technologies. SMEs can connect to 5G networks using the Internet and enjoy the benefit of greater bandwidth and super-fast download speeds of up to 10 gigabits per second. 5G will introduce SMEs to capabilities such as the Internet of things (IoT) and non-human-based machine-to-machine (M2M) communication. For those operating SME businesses, it is predicted that 5G will transform human and technology relations and systems in unpredictable ways by default. Indeed Verbeek (2005) has observed that "human beings not as unique individuals but as fulfillers of functions who are in principle interchangeable" (p 18).

3.3.1. Information Systems Security and Cybersecurity in SMEs in Early Days

Steady growth in technology usage gave rise to information systems security and cybersecurity. It was during the 1960s when businesses started realizing that they needed to protect access to their computers. As the Internet had not yet gained traction during this time, the most appropriate form of access control was physical, where users were physically prevented access. The 1961 Compatible Time-Sharing System (CTSS) at the Massachusetts Institute of Technology (MIT) was likely the first to deploy access control that was not physical and involved the use of passwords (Bonneau, Herley, Van Oorschot, & Stajano, 2015). This novel development seemed to precipitate security concerns immediately as cases started being reported of users attempting access by guessing each other's passwords. There were also reported leaks on the master password file (Bonneau, 2015). Back then, these files were not encrypted. Then there was Multics, or the 'Multiplexed Information and Computing Service,' an advanced time-sharing operating system that was intended to provide simultaneous user access using remote terminals similar to MIT's CTSS. What was new was that Multics could protect sensitive data using passwords stored in hashed form (Sibert & Baldwin, 2007).

During the late 1980s and early 1990s, businesses and computer users faced more advanced methods of password guessing bringing information and cybersecurity into the limelight. The 1988 Moris Internet worm showed the weakness of storing passwords in hash form, and administrators realized it was better to store password files in heavily protected shadow files (Spafford, 1989). With the growth of the World Wide Web and e-Commerce in the late 1990s, attempts were made to replace passwords with public-key cryptography. More robust password protection was possible by using protocols to send data electronically, using electronic transaction (SET) protocol, and protecting such data via a secure sockets layer (SSL) (Bonneau, 2015).

Because of advanced persistent threats from hackers, modern SMEs have developed advanced forms of password improvements and access controls using many available guidelines. One such popular guideline comes from the National Institute of Standards and Technology (NIST) framework for cybersecurity solutions aimed at helping businesses manage and reduce cybersecurity risk. For example, in the case of password improvement, the NIST guideline proposes increasing password strength by increasing the minimum length, expanding the classes of characters used, and having at least one character in uppercase and one that is non-alphabetic. Besides the focus on passwords, other major evolutions have occurred in information and cybersecurity. These are discussed in the next section.

3.3.2. Major Evolution in Information Systems Security and Cybersecurity in SMEs during and after COVID-19

The coronavirus pandemic, popularly known as COVID-19, presented SMEs with unique challenges not previously experienced. With most SMEs required to shut down, many moved to the virtual cyber-space to remain operational. This move opened up another new challenge. Many SMEs were not skilled or savvy enough to know the kinds and types of cyber-security threats present in the cyber-space. It was no surprise that a rise in cyber-threats to SMEs occurred during this period.

Many SMEs had not been technically savvy to prioritize cyber-security, and attacks started. Research work done by security professionals presents insightful data that shows that at the peak periods of the COVID-19 initiated lockdowns, cybersecurity incidents targeting SMEs such as phishing, pharming, and financial fraud and extortion increased (Lallie et al., 2021). Many professional experts agree that this period was unique because many people were required to work from home. Thrill-seekers and those with enough computer skills suddenly had more free time and opportunities to perform nefarious computer-based acts. What is also interesting is that during this time, progressively innovative novel attacks occurred. Novel attacks presented unique challenges to SMEs.

Recorded cyber-crimes increased during the peak period of Covid19 lockdowns in the UK, affecting SMEs and impacting the cost of doing business (Buil-Gil, Miró-Llinares, Moneva, Kemp, & Díaz-Castaño, 2021). Documented breaches from illegal remote access included breaches of personal health information and theft of personally identifiable information malware (Muthuppalaniappan & Stevenson, 2021). SMEs also experienced an increase in phishing email attacks targeted at business owners who intended to access privileged information such as bank account records (Georgiadou, Mouzakitis, & Askounis, 2021).

3.3.3. Major Evolution in Cybersecurity Software Hardware and Networking Evolution in SMEs

Malicious software (malware) continues to affect many SMEs, and many SMEs now report on new forms of malware that are more sophisticated and increasingly targeting specific SME applications that can now evade anti-malware software (van Haastrecht et al., 2021). Modern malware now has the capability of not only evading traditional defense mechanisms for networked computers but such malware now has the capability of accessing sensitive data (Armenia, Angelini, Nonino, Palombi, & Schlitzer, 2021).

Many SMEs are now encouraged to be proactive, evolve in tandem with evolving threats, and move from the old ways of protecting themselves from cyber-security threats. SME owner-managers can now deploy modern technology-centric advanced endpoint malware detection and response tools as an example of a modern security threat mitigation strategy (Emer, Unterhofer, & Rauch, 2021). Without taking such measures, SMEs using computer-based microprocessors may be subjected to security threats from malware such as Meltdown and Spectre, identified by Google's Project Zero, which can allow programs to steal data processed using these microprocessors (Smith & Curran, 2021, p. 27).

According to Smith and Curran (2021, p. 27), Spectre is a malware that can "exploit speculative execution to access data stored in protective memory store that lives next to memory allocated" to the malware. Reports show that cybercrimes will continue to be persistent, targeting SMEs, which are seen as an easy soft target because SME owner-managers may not have adequately addressed security risks by taking necessary safeguards. (Auyporn, Piromsopa, & Chaiyawat, 2020). As new practices evolve, new sets of policies will be created which can enable proper governance of these threats by SMEs. The governance of cybersecurity threats is discussed in the next section.

3.4. Information Systems Security Governance Evolution

A study on SMEs revealed that most SME owner-managers believe that an increase in successful cyber-security attacks on their businesses is imminent. Cyber-security attacks on SMEs have grown in sophistication. As long as SMEs remain soft targets by cyber-criminals, Owner-managers of these SMEs should be expected to adopt new practices to cyber-security governance in light of these threat advancements and should not see cyber-security as a big business only concern (Bell, 2017). Failure to do so may mean that cyber-attacks on SMEs' computing assets will continue unabated. To start, SME owner-managers should re-strategize and prioritize cyber-security governance investment initiatives by fostering a continuous and dedicated cyber-security incident monitoring initiative. SME owner-managers should take a leading role in re-skilling and training themselves and those they employ to prepare for innovative attacks on their systems. The nature of cybersecurity governance is changing, and the owner-managers of SMEs are encouraged to change their management approaches in response to these changes.

For the SMEs concerned, cyber-security governance should involve a unified and coordinated approach at the management level to initiate cybersecurity governance programs, such as introducing policies, strategies, and goals for cyber-security risk mitigation. Furthermore, owner-managers must access cybersecurity risks and determine how these risks may impact business operations, and initiate mechanisms for continuous monitoring of cybersecurity risks. Cybersecurity governance initiatives must be placed on the SME, knowing that focus and directions must come from the owner-manager, who should remain constantly engaged and committed to cybersecurity risk mitigation initiatives. Owner-managers can request assistance from more specialized practitioners and collaborate with other SMEs in policy-making, raising awareness, and other cybersecurity initiatives.

3.5. Conclusion

This chapter has argued that in pursuit of competitiveness in a changing global economy, SMEs have evolved and adopted technologies innovatively, with rapid evolution witnessed during and after the outbreak of the COVID-19 pandemic. The following are key points that the chapter presents.

Key Points

- 4IR is characterized by innovative technologies such as 5G, IoT, big data, AI, and machine learning.
- SMEs need to be competitive in the era of 4IR and adopt newer technologies to remain relevant as 4IR continues to disrupt transitional operations.
- There are embedded information and cybersecurity risks in using these 4IR technologies that owner-managers of SMEs need to take cognizance of.
- The COVID-19 pandemic accelerated the use of these technologies, such as Zoom and MS teams, for communication, but the unintended consequence was that these technologies became targets for cyberattacks.
- Effective cybersecurity governance is required of SMEs to mitigate cyber-attacks in the era of 4IR.

Chapter 4

Information Systems Security Behavior and Culture in SMEs

4.1. Introduction

The first three chapters of this book have presented a more profound understanding of the cybersecurity threats and challenge SMEs face as they continue to digitize their operations. Technology change and evolution have presented SMEs with more critical and unique considerations not previously envisaged by owner-mangers of SMEs. In the process, technology change has created essential disruptions to the traditional way SMEs operate. As suggested in Chapter 3, SMEs inevitably adapt to these technology changes to remain relevant and survive the competition.

This chapter addresses an important area of cybersecurity that is commonly instinctive and less discussed, namely behavior and culture. Both seemingly have a significant impact on the ability of owner-managers of SMEs to adapt to technology change and are partly why many SMEs fail to adapt to technological change and struggle to remain competitive. Section 4.1 considers culture and behavior while Section 4.2 focusses of insider behavior as a threat to information security. Section 4.3 discusses how positive behavior may be encouraged.

The old maxim that 'culture eats strategy for breakfast' holds for well-intended owner-managers of SMEs visionary enough to steer their business operations to more competitive levels. Their strategic efforts often fail for the very reason that SME culture is a stumbling block. Indeed, studies present us with alarming statistics which show that 70% - 80% of SMEs fail within the first two years of business operation (Erasmus, Reynolds, & Fourie, 2019). Culture and behavior have been attributed as crucial reasons. The impact of these two on cybersecurity threat mitigation is addressed in the following section.

4.2. Culture and Behavior in SMEs Operations and Impact to Cybersecurity Threat Mitigation

When employees move from one location to the next, what follows them is their own cultural and behavioral values. At the same time, they are likely to abandon any institutional values they previously held (Liu, 2014). The cultural and behavioral values they present to new institutions or work environments will often influence those in these new environments and will often form part of new cultures that may impact the cybersecurity posture of an SME. Sound security policies may be ineffective without a proper way of cultivating a positive culture. It is therefore vital for SME owner-managers to understand what information security culture is. According to Nel and Drevin (2019), information security culture is considered a subculture of any organizational culture and becomes embedded as part of the broad organizational functions in the long run. It is from this perspective that many would argue that information security culture should therefore be grounded in and become complementary to fostering enterprise-wise positive cultural efforts.

The culture of employees is closely tied to the way they behave within the workplace. If this is positive behavior, such as making information security a natural part of the way daily a task is carried out, then such conduct has an enterprise-wide benefit. For example, when an employee is granted access to a system, they must use strong passwords. The reason for this is that modern computerized tools easily compromise weak passwords. Employees may belittle this policy to the detriment of the entire organization when out of laziness or inadvertency, they choose to use weak passwords or even share their passwords with others. Such negative behavior should often be discouraged. Studies have shown that there are alternatives to passwords, such as biometric authentication or voice recognition, but because of cultural and behavioral values, many employees still prefer using passwords (Schlienger & Teufel, 2002).

According to Afolayan and de la Harpe (2020), behavior and culture may impact SMEs' strategic decision-making regarding the use and usefulness of diverse technologies. This ultimately impacts how SMEs perform, how efficient they become, and importantly, how they leverage their competitive advantage. From the perspective of Govender and Pretorius (2015), SMEs are less motivated when compared to their larger counterparts adapting to IT. The reasoning is not necessarily anchored on IT costs, ease of use, or even usefulness of IT, but instead on behavioral and cultural predispositions. This primarily means that SMEs' perception of applying IT to mitigate cybersecurity threats may be hindered. This goes against current competitive business trends.

For businesses attempting to develop an influential information security culture, requisite knowledge amongst employees is necessary, with shared tacit assumptions and espoused values playing a leading role in shaping SMEs' cybersecurity maturity (Van Niekerk & Von Solms, 2010).

Academic studies have addressed culture and behavior from vantage points, such as when employees may choose whether to comply or not with information security policies designed for the organization's benefit (Chen et al., 2021). Accountability theory, for example, draws on a perspective that considers the positive action/reaction which determines how that employee will behave and the role they will play in reducing the need to violate an information security policy (Vance, Lowry, & Eggett, 2015). Other studies on behavior and moral hazards address activities such as when employees use technologies and computers to hide computer activities (Lowry, Posey, Roberts, & Bennett, 2014). Some studies have proposed that culture and behavior can be influenced by constructs such as balancing fairness and trust to encourage employees to follow sound information security practices (Lowry, Posey, Bennett, & Roberts, 2015). An important consideration to note regarding how culture and behavior shape the information and cybersecurity posture of an SME is that owner-managers of SMEs will require a better understanding of how these two can be used to help SMEs apply information and cybersecurity initiatives much better.

4.3. The Role of the Insider as a Security Threat

Closely tied to holistic organizational behavior is considering the behavior of an individual employee who has a high degree of access and trust in SME systems. The behavior of an employee (often referred to as an insider) with such privileges is crucial to the information and cybersecurity posture of an SME because this privileged access can enable such an employee to perform both authorized and unauthorized functions such as abusing systems. Positive behavior outcomes may be shaped by designing control measures using password authorization that allows for a middle ground where sufficient privileges are granted while malevolent usage is mitigated (Dini & Lopriore, 2015). SMEs should strive to track their insider's access to what could be deemed confidential information, ensuring that proper procedures, guidelines, and policies are kept in order to detect and prevent any unauthorized use of such information.

While it may be challenging to monitor and construe the intention of every employee, it has been shown that many insiders become a threat to the business when there is a perceived gain or the insider is disgruntled (Georgiadou, Mouzakitis, & Askounis, 2021). Being overzealousness to get the job, as well as stress or exacerbated factors outside the work environment such as family issues, are behavioral traits that owner-managers should always be on alert for, as these have been shown to impact SME's information security posture (Sarkar, 2010).

4.4. Building Positive Cybersecurity Behavior and Culture in SMEs

The need for owner-managers and those seen in positions of authority to build and encourage positive cybersecurity culture cannot be underestimated. Encouraging a positive mindset change on the part of employees is necessary since there are now many regulations and legislations that require this to be done. Legislation such as the General Data Protection Regulation (GDPR) has been attributed to catalyzing a mindset change and promoting positive cybersecurity behavior.

Many frameworks created to improve behavior and culture are often oriented toward big businesses, with many proposed factors lacking in SMEs. As a result, SME owner-managers struggle to build positive cybersecurity culture and behavior by taking initiatives to develop clear policies and procedures for employees to follow. Positive behavior may be encouraged, for instance, by deleting the privileges of employees when they betray the trust given (Baracaldo & Joshi, 2013). Now, technologies on hand can generate access exemptions in real-time when employees' actions are considered inappropriate. These technologies are embedded with a privilege management mechanism that will integrate risks and trust against any emergent insider threat, as shown in Table 5.

Table 5. Useful control habits

Framework	Basis	Source
Corporate culture model	The three levels of corporate culture that include artifacts, espoused values and shared tacit assumptions should be supported by the fourth level of information security knowledge.	Van Niekerk & Von Solms, (2010)
STOPE framework	STOPE includes Strategy, technology, organization, people, and environment acts as a building block to build and guide the development of a security culture, while addressing preparedness, responsibility management and regulations.	Al Hogail, (2015)
Information Security Culture Change Framework	Focuses on fostering positive information security culture through cultivating good behavior and integrating change management principles while examining human elements.	AlHogail & Mirza, (2014)
ARCS Framework	Considers information security risk, Assessment of, the Reduction of Cost and the Sustainability of information security culture	Govender, Kritzinger, & Loock, (2020)

Owner-mangers of SMEs should not follow these frameworks, which rigidly advocate for positive information security culture but foster attempts to draw on these insights to cultivate bespoke needs. When owner-managers consider inclusive information security cultural needs for SMEs, many of these frameworks vary and may not be applicable in all SME contexts. SMEs are better off pursuing multiple approaches which can be tailored as needed. Owner-managers can identify employees who can design, test, and evaluate custom-made information security culture approaches that can stand emerging and changing cultural and regulatory requirements. In an approach to design better policies, owner-managers should address some of the problems that would foster positive culture change as follows:

4.4.1. Building Positive Cybersecurity Behavior by Making Procedures More Usable

Employees often complain that information and cybersecurity policies are challenging to follow or even unusable because these are seen as foreign to SMEs' local needs. Owner-managers of SMEs should be encouraged to design policies and procedures based on actual activities carried out within the SMEs using employees' perspectives and not from technical manuals or perspectives that are foreign. Owner-managers can encourage employees to co-create a better information security culture within their SMEs.

4.4.2. Raising Awareness of the Risks of Using Technologies

Many employees working in SMEs do not understand the risks associated with using computerized, networked technologies. The risk increases with new technologies such as smartphones, the Internet of Things (IoT), cloud computing, and artificial intelligence. Owner-managers of SMEs should formally inform employees about these risks by fostering a training and awareness culture through period training and sensitization campaigns.

4.4.3. Designing Security Measures and Techniques That Are Easy to Understand

When attempting to design security measures and techniques, owner-managers should ensure that these measures are well-intended and will not stifle work. If work is stifled because of these measures, this may produce unintended consequences of workarounds. One primary reason for these unintended consequences is that employees of SMEs do not understand these information security measures. It is therefore advisable that these measures are communicated, made explicating, and a system to monitor and remind employees that such measures carry significant weight be instituted.

4.4.4. Addressing Instances When the Employee Becomes an Information Security Risk

Employees may not consider themselves involved in SME security initiatives, which could be detrimental to their overall security posture. These employees may be distant from the overall SME values and goals and may ultimately become a risk to the SMEs. Owner-managers are encouraged to partner with these employees and remind them that they are co-creators of SME security initiatives. Part of addressing employee risks is to draw up explicit information security agreements with the employees that address the proper behavior the employee should have when handling information.

4.5. Conclusion

This chapter has discussed the prevailing information security culture and behavior that characterizes the running of SMEs. The primary concern is the role an insider (employee of an SME) as a security threat plays. The following are key points that the chapter presents.

Key Points

- Behavior and culture can influence how SMEs address information and cybersecurity risk.
- Negative behavior, culture and habits can exacerbate information and cybersecurity risk posture of SMEs.
- SMEs insiders can be part of information and cybersecurity threat to SMEs if poorly managed and SMEs need to be cognizant of this.
- There are various frameworks that can be applied by SMEs to foster better behavior and overall culture of information and cybersecurity compliance.

Chapter 5

Information Systems Security and the Role of Women Entrepreneurs in SMEs

5.1. Introduction

As the information security and cybersecurity profession matures, the sector is still seen as a non-traditional career front for many women. There are still relatively few women in the field. However, some proactive women have set up initiatives to break down well-established barriers by establishing initiatives such as women's support centers. These initiatives have gained traction, with Cisco, the global IT, and networking company noting growth in the representation of women in career choices such as engineering, consulting, and entrepreneurship. The purpose of this chapter is to highlight women's initiatives and the advocacy of better female representation in the information security and cybersecurity profession. Section 5.1 addresses the role of women's entrepreneurship and the challenges women have faced. Section 5.2 highlights how women have broken the barrier, with many having thriving cybersecurity and Section 5.3 discusses information security careers for women. Section 5.4 addresses educational opportunities for women in SMEs. This section focuses on the cybersecurity aspects of SMEs and the education opportunities available.

5.2. Equity, Diversity and Inclusion for Career Women

The advocacy for better female representation in career fields in science, technology, engineering, and mathematics (STEM), has not been easy. A while back, a study by Beyer, Rynes, and Haller (2004) addressed the many concerns and deterrents to women in computer science courses. The most recent study by Vooren, Haelermans, Groot, and van den Brink (2022) shows that females are less likely to enroll in STEM-related fields, coupled with concern that female students are less likely to graduate than men within the nominal duration. This translates into a lower female representation in technology companies, with even fewer women taking up technical leadership roles.

The United Nations marks 'The International Day of Women and Girls in Science' every year on February 11. The theme for 2022 was 'Gender Equality Today for a Sustainable Tomorrow', whose primary objective is to highlight the role of STEM in improving water and sanitation across the globe. Significant global women-driven initiates, such as Luisa Ulrici, a female physicist from CERN's Environmental Protection group showcasing her work to a mixed-class primary school in Saint-Genis-Pouilly, France, in February 11, 2022 (Samson, 2022). These United Nations initiatives push for the assistance of leading women innovators and those in solid science and technology fields to offer innovative solutions to many of the problems faced by society. Indeed, we can start seeing women playing a pivotal role in this year's theme regarding water security innovation (Tang, 2022).

5.3. Women Entrepreneurs in SMEs

A study by Wellalage and Locke (2017) found that women entrepreneurs in Asia running women-owned SMEs faced access to credit constraints. The main reason women continue to face entrepreneurial struggle is anchored on the following: Firstly, women face 'taste discrimination.' Taste discrimination can materialize when financial systems issuing credit are primarily male-dominated. Secondly, women face 'statistical discrimination', where women tend to have a lower degree of education and involvement in formal market economies.

5.3.1. Financing Technology and Entrepreneurial Struggle

A study of SMEs in South-East Asia examined credit constraints between male and female entrepreneurs showing that that it is crucial not to introduce policies that may favor women-only SMEs regarding credit access and pricing. This is because this may create unwanted incentives for women to remain small with resources being directed towards competitively low-value creation.

Like South-East Asia, sub-Sahara Africa also faces a gender imbalance in access to credit by women. Hansen and Rand (2014) showed that SMEs where there is female ownership participation, these SMEs tend to be of smaller size and the idea that smaller SMEs, on average, tend to be constrained in access to formal financing and credit (Aterido, Beck, & Iacovone, 2013). Indeed, according to Aterido et al., (2013), there is evidence that women entrepreneurs have had to overcome selection biases, barriers to innovation, and access to financial resources. Selection bias prevails since men control most financing businesses, disadvantaging many women. Besides selection bias, women will face challenges such as deleterious socio-cultural attitudes as they run SMEs.

For most SMEs owned and managed by women, access to financial credit is difficult since many women do not have collateral and have fewer financial assets than men. The paradox is that women-managed SMEs are stable. If given credit, many women perform better and post higher credit turnover than men in businesses run by men. Women's positive contribution has not gone unnoticed, and the private sector and governments are beginning to recognize the importance women-owned SMEs are providing to the economy. On this basis, government and private-sector-driven initiatives to support women SMEs are gaining traction. For women-owned SMEs, private and government sector initiatives can support SMEs by providing information and training about finance, such as writing business proposals for funding and managing finances once the credit is granted.

In support of women's entrepreneurship in South Africa, Google, a U.S.-based multinational IT, pledged R15.3 million in charitable funds. It is estimated that close to 58% of SMEs in South Africa are run by women entrepreneurs who are disadvantaged in obtaining access to financing in formal channels such as banks, which place stringent requirements. Google has also provided free online tools such as Google Business Profiles to help SMEs run by women benefit from its pool of technical resources to help women grow their businesses. Such tools can help women entrepreneurs discover themselves and the businesses they run and, importantly, support each other.

5.3.2. Overcoming Fear of Failure by Women Entrepreneurs

Women will better embrace support from the government and the private sector because they tend to fear failure than men. This fear can inhibit successful entrepreneurial resourcefulness and may most likely lead to them not being willing to borrow and own an SME. Women are encouraged to teach and learn from other's women support groups and, in doing so, to drive away from this fear. Women support groups tend to foster commitment and confidence, especially when they see their fellow women are successful. The networking in these support groups creates inertia that can attract motivational speakers to talk of context-specific problems supporting women SMEs. This can be achieved and yield better results when women identify established and successful women role models as speakers. Women support groups foster credibility and accountability because women can start appreciating each other's efforts, and through this, trust is established. Trust is an essential component of attracting the much-needed financing of SMEs. Trust can be better built-in women's support groups and networks than in male-dominated communities.

5.3.3. Gender and Information Security Behavior

Women are beginning to play an essential role in touching on organizations' perceptions, attitudes, and performance of information security activities. Studies have long assumed that gender differences are important considerations for technology adoption and use in workplaces (Morris, Venkatesh, & Ackerman, 2005). Recent studies confirm that women self-reported differently, with men reporting better cybersecurity behavior, with men were over-confident in cybersecurity, skills experience, cues-to-action, and general security behavior (Anwar et al., 2017).

Many governments worldwide strive to promote equal access to economic development activities and reduce income and other gender-based inequalities by ensuring equal opportunities through affirmative action campaigns. Although there is evidence that affirmative action is gaining traction globally, one seemingly lagging area is access to information and computing technology (Vimalkumar, Singh, & Gouda, 2021).

According to the Economist Intelligence Unit report, it is estimated that men accessing the Internet is 80.2 percent higher than women in low-income countries, with only 29 percent of internet users being women (Vimalkumar et al., 2021).

5.4. Women in Information Security and Cybersecurity Profession

Because IT and ICT are considered an avenue for development-based initiatives and an enabler of entrepreneurship, unequal access to the skills that would enable women to play a meaningful role remains a challenge. Moreover, the ability of women running small businesses to obtain the skills necessary to protect these against any IT or ICT-driven attack would be hampered.

5.4.1. Marriage and IT Career Women

In most developing countries, marriage will play an essential role in the life and career of a woman because prevailing values and social norms will dictate the responsibilities of a woman. On the one hand, a married man is expected to bear the role of a family head, bearing the responsibility for the needs of a family. On the other hand, a woman is expected to concentrate on household duties, including rearing children and caring for and cooking. A woman seeking to advance her career will often find this challenging and, in most instances, will invest more in the needs of the family and husband at the expense of her career growth. Those women choosing to balance the needs of advancing their professional careers would do so, bearing in mind that they would still have to fulfill their household duties. The professional would therefore have to navigate between household duties, her professional work, and significantly advancing her skills through specialized education.

5.4.2. Women in IT and Cybersecurity

According to Morgan (2019), the notion of 'cyber' alludes to a 'gender problem.' The concern raised is that in 2013 women made up only 11 percent of the entire global cybersecurity workforce, and six years later, women made up 20 percent of the workforce. This is a marginal but encouraging development. It should be seen that besides computer security, which offers cybersecurity training, other STEM professions suffer the same fate because young women have shunned STEM-related fields, and many still do. There is a persistent stereotype that STEM is a preserve of men. This is at the backdrop of studies showing that women consistently score well or even better than men on math and other science-related tests.

There are attempts by organizations to address the gender bias outlined by Morgan (2019). Young women often formulate preconceptions regarding the choices they have in their careers and the future role they will play, which often limit the full extent of choices they have. Even though media has played an essential role towards positive change and contribution, women keep providing in math and science careers. The young women will view career choices such as cybersecurity as requiring them to be much more accomplished than men to get equal treatment, perhaps. Media and Hollywood, which portray cybersecurity and ethical hacking as tasks having war and military connotations more suitable for men, often reinforce women's preconceptions about cybersecurity.

Women have unique attributes that can be of value to the cybersecurity profession such as their naturally endowed ability to nurture. This ability can make most endure under challenging circumstances better than men do. In many instances, women can multitask better, such as obtain academic qualifications while nurturing their young ones and taking responsibility for household chores. This also means that they are better at finding solutions to unsolved problems. These qualities can be extended to the cybersecurity profession and can bring value and a positive impact to the profession. Notwithstanding, the increase in female participation across global universities in the cybersecurity profession has been made possible by online access, making women work, learn, and at the same time balance and manage their private lives better.

The highlighting of the cybersecurity profession is now more accessible online, enabling better participation, better privacy awareness, and the understanding of the digital threats of day-to-day life. Women may use their multitasking abilities and train other women in the cybersecurity field, explaining to others the endless possibilities the career may present and, more importantly, how financially empowering these opportunities are.

The ability to multitask is vital in this age where many women experience technology disruption. Since women are primarily risk-averse, getting into the cybersecurity profession would be coherent with their natural ability to seek security. Many see the need for security in whatever form is inbuilt into women's DNA. Women choose to study security-related courses because they want to be effective and affect the world they live in strategically and positively (Triana, Miller, & Trzebiatowski, 2014).

Women's natural desire to protect people is a pull factor for women to venture into the cybersecurity and information security space. Indeed, the profession of information and cybersecurity is embedded with these same principles: to not only protect people but, importantly, their information, as well as the safety of transacting online. Similarly, a woman in the cybersecurity profession is more likely to impress and influence another by inculcating a natural desire to model a successful fellow woman's career choices. Since cybersecurity requires the professional to constantly communicate new security threats that many impact organizations adversely, the communication skills natural to women may endear them to this profession. Many see women as better communicators that understand business risk and are more resilient.

When organizations understand this, these organizations can design women-driven and bespoke recruitment strategies that make cybersecurity more accessible and inclusive to women. For example, inclusivity may take the form of bespoke women-driven communication, tailored penetration testing methods that women can understand, and fostering collegial information security awareness and training in exciting ways.

From a cybersecurity training perspective, the most popular approach has been hackathons, which are special training events that last between 24 and 48 hours. These events are trendy in bringing cybersecurity and those interested in the profession, such as designers, software engineers, and social educators, to obtain new skills quickly when creating new projects from scratch. There are, however, concerns that there is low participation amongst women generally (Paganini & Gama, 2020). Some women may naturally prefer working on longer-term projects rather than sitting down on one short project for between 24 and 48 hours, making hackathon participation minimal. Other women may find the idea of working in a hackathon environment very distracting and impeding focus and motivation, which can be counterproductive. Some women have even suggested that the hackathon space is often crowded and full of clutter, filled with laptops and food all over the place, with hackathon participants staying up all night on the floor catching up on late hours of sleep. The whole idea of a hackathon can be daunting and may put off women's keep to learning cybersecurity skills (Paganini & Gama, 2020).

5.4.3. Possible Cybersecurity Routes Women Can Pursue

Most women may not know that the cybersecurity profession has various career routes that can be pursued and that cybersecurity is not limited to either ethical hacking or cryptography. Women can pursue fields such as identity management, data privacy in SMEs, how SMEs can benefit from the Internet of Things (IoT) technologies, and fields such as digital security.

In a report published by Cybersecurity-Guide (2021), women who choose cybersecurity as a profession tend to leave this profession in a higher proportion than men, in often relatively short order. Some reasons are possible that women feel left out or marginalized socially in what may be seen as a boys' club atmosphere or the perceived intensity of the career. Perhaps the reality is that generally, women tend to be paid less than men in similar tasks, with promotions far between making women less motivated and comfortable in such workspaces (Cybersecurity-Guide, 2021).

There are workplace programs that encourage diversity, which can apply to women owning and managing SMEs. Diversity in disciplines, skills, gender, and ethnicity can ensure a fresh perspective in promoting creativity and innovation. Women need to be skilled in this area to manage or be sought after in cybersecurity recruitment efforts. The focus should then be on how women are educated in this space and how the discipline of cybersecurity is taught to women.

5.5. Educating Women in Information and Cybersecurity

Most women seek to be fulfilled in their roles and duties and not just defined by what culture and social norms dictate. Many seek meaningful work that often gives them a sense of purpose. It is not a surprise then that increasingly, many women are being encouraged to pursue careers in the science, technology, engineering, and mathematics (STEM) fields. Currently, according to the National Girls Collaborative Project, only 17.9 percent of girls receive computer science degrees in the United States (Hoffman & Friedman, 2018).

Few women graduate in degrees such as computer science and IT, which are foundations for successful careers in information and cybersecurity, may not bode well for the future of women in entrepreneurship in SMEs. They can shape and define policies and governance in the field. There is evidence that an essential ingredient for better business productivity is creativity that is anchored on diversity. Homogenous groupings such as male-dominated workplaces that influence information security policy and governance will not be as effective as that of a diverse group of people (Friedman, Friedman, & Leverton, 2016). Therefore, it is necessary to include women to foster creativity and collective intelligence that shows that the business is socially sensitive. Indeed, Thompson (2015, p. 1) suggests that;

> "A general collective intelligence factor explains a group performance on various tasks. This "c factor" is not strongly correlated with group members' average or maximum individual intelligence. However, it is correlated with the average social sensitivity of group members, the equality in distribution of conversational turn-taking, and the proportion of females in the group." (Thompson, 2015)

The benefit of women's "c factor" suggests that women can do some things better than men, and indeed Thompson (2015, p. 1) agreed that;

> "Women are better at reading the mind through the face even online when they cannot see their teammates' face." (Thompson, 2015)

A study by the University of Wisconsin-Parkside showed that women tended to value their professional careers more than men (Beyer et al., 2004). The study showed that women are more inclined to pursue careers that help others. The same study showed that these women did not realize that a career in computer science could also help others. For this reason, many would shy away from it. Many women did not know that not only would computer science provide a sense of purpose and a meaningful career, but it was also applied in many industries to help people. A woman pursuing a computer science degree would find purpose and perform meaningful work providing services that help numerous people. A woman pursuing a profession in information and cybersecurity may help fight against cybercriminals. Recruiting such a woman would be to the advantage of businesses that include SMEs. In addition, women computer scientists can help protect organizations such as SMEs in meaningful and life-fulfilling ways. In a speech in February 2013, meant to motivate more women into STEM careers, the then President Barak Obama said as follows;

> "One of the things that I really strongly believe in is that we need to have more girls interested in math, science, and engineering. We have

got half the population that is way underrepresented in those fields, and that means that we have got a whole bunch of talent, not being encouraged the way they need to." (Hoffman & Friedman, 2018)

5.5.1. Certification and Formal Education for Women in Cybersecurity

It is crucial for education providers in the information and cybersecurity space to promote Cybersecurity as a desirable career option for women and make it available in a broad of offerings such as short certificate courses, formal degrees, and diplomas, as well as advanced certification and executive education programs depending on the needs of the women. There are a few industry-standard certifications in Cybersecurity available to women entrepreneurs and SME owners. These standards include Certified Information Systems Security Professional (CISSP) and Certified Information System Auditor (CISA).

Information Systems Audit and Control Association (ISACA) is a professional body developing these standards. It can help women get back into the field of Cybersecurity with relevant and updated skillsets. These initiatives will create a promising pipeline for women to be recruited into organizations and, importantly, for the women entrepreneurs to run successful SMEs.

As suggested by Cybersecurity-Guide (2021), it seems that women who pursue studying other disciplines beyond IT and computer science may also be good candidates for both information security and Cybersecurity. As long as sufficient certification training within these areas complements what the women have studied, this path may provide a leg up in enabling women to find their way into Cybersecurity. Institutions of training may also provide access to young professional women studying in these areas to those in the industry.

5.5.2. Entrepreneurial Role of Women in Cybersecurity

Women entrepreneurs contribute to global GDP in equal proportion to men, and the GDP would ultimately increase by 3 percent to 6 percent by USD 2.5 trillion to USD 5 trillion, respectively, in 2020 (Khan, 2020). In most places globally, it is estimated that the early-stage participation by women entrepreneurs running SMEs is half or less than that of male entrepreneurs (Khan, 2020). While there remains a massive shortage, of women in the cybersecurity, profession owning or managing SME startups, wealthy businesses can make available resources such as technology skills, financial support, networking, and entrepreneurship training. The drive toward venture capitalists supporting women-dedicated SME startups and accelerated programs requires sustenance. These initiatives can propel GDP growth where women-owned SMEs may provide fresh ideas and innovation of products and services that generate traction in developing cybersecurity careers for women.

A notable initiative was in 2019 when the United States (US) government launched the 'Women's Global Development and Prosperity initiative' (Khan, 2020). The purpose was to support over 50 million women in the developing world until 2025 and is built on the pillars of women's prosperity in workplaces, women succeeding as entrepreneurs, and having women who are enabled and co-contributors of economic growth just like men.

5.5.3. Women in Cybersecurity Working from Home

The rise of the gig economy, a common term to refer to a free-market system that advocates for the hiring of independent workers for short-term projects, has been on the rise empowering many women (Onyejekwe, 2011). This is significantly sorer in the advent of the COVID-19 pandemic. The gig economy has attracted a significant number of women into the cybersecurity field as the growth of the Internet has opened up a window for empowering women globally. Many new refer to the tech gig economy as the "new normal."

Although it is said that working remotely from home is not new (Nilles, 1976), this idea has recently generated significant interest amongst information security researchers in light of the COVID-19 pandemic. Many countries face working restrictions such as social distancing and global lockdowns that have disrupted everyday work routines. Many organizations have, however, discovered that there are benefits to these new remote work arrangements because they can better access a wider pool of specialized information security and cybersecurity talent pool. This pool of specialized people can solve organizational problems remotely and without working full-time.

The field of cybersecurity fits well for this gig economy model, particularly for talented independent women working in small businesses at home. Women will have the flexibility and occasion to choose exciting projects at the convenience of their homes. Many opportunities are available to address cybersecurity problems for women who choose to work from home.

Women can take advantage of the changing nature of technology to provide solutions for information and cybersecurity threats and vulnerabilities since many institutions are presently online. Many online institutions may not have placed the proper risk control measures on their employees working from home (Bispham, Creese, Dutton, Esteve-Gonzalez, & Goldsmith, 2021). From the point of view of organizations, these changes have introduced vulnerabilities that make online assets reachable, amplifying the threats because of the increased dependency on using the Internet to continue business operations (Bispham et al., 2021). The dependency on the Internet has given rise to more cybersecurity incidents such as debit or credit card fraud, online identity theft, loss of business information and data due to phishing and pharming attacks, viruses and malware infections, and even misuse of personal information available on the net.

For women running small businesses and developing an interest in practicing in the cybersecurity profession from home, it is paramount that they are skilled enough and have invested in a stable Internet connection. Moreover, women must take cognizance of the eroding of boundaries between work and private time, as the devices used when working from home continually connect to the Internet. This means they must be ready to work at odd hours, knowing well that the traditional household hoe was in many cases never designed for working from home. Women must therefore build bespoke environments that are friendly to work and living spaces while avoiding distractions from family members.

One caveat that should be advocated for women choosing to work from home is that, from an information security perspective, many mistakes can be made at home that would otherwise be counterproductive. These mistakes can manifest when the workspace at home is vulnerable and potentially create information security problems. Vulnerability at home could be not correctly configuring the home's virtual private network (VPN) or placing too much rust on vendor-specified security configuration for a home workspace.

It is also crucial for women working from home to ensure they have invested in proper anti-virus software and software that can detect and prevent intrusion of the home workspace systems. Using connected devices in the home workspace such as phones, laptops, tablets, printers, and even home cameras (web-cams) designated as the Internet of Things (IoT) may create multiple vulnerable areas of attack from external threats at the home workspace. It should be noted that the home workspace is essentially not a trusted environment to work on. This may create complacency for women traditionally used to working in offices where the environment was more trusted. In trusted environments, access to specific resources and links would, for instance, be restricted because of threats such as phishing attacks. At home and in workspaces, this configuration would be different. Women can use newer technologies called 'zero-trust systems' that move the security control such as authentication away from a perimeter such as a home workspace to serve in the cloud. From a cybersecurity perspective, women should also be cautious when sensitizing others about cybersecurity threats. At the same time, they might not be adhering to security control measures such as using private infrastructure and allowing other family members to connect to the same infrastructure and router. Once a small home cybersecurity practice has been set up, women can determine the service-pricing model; choose exciting (and sometimes not-so-exciting projects) as opportunities come. Women should continually upskill so as not to become redundant while realizing that practicing cybersecurity at home can be, at times, lonely and demanding. There are still very few women cybersecurity professionals and even fewer women professionals practicing in their home spaces. Perhaps this is why the advocacy for women in the profession should be strengthened.

5.5.4. Protecting Women Entrepreneurs in SMEs

Women face continuous harassment, occupation segregation, and even violence at the workplace and need to be protected. It is in the backdrop of these conditions the United Nation's Sustainable Development Goal (SDG) 5 seeks to eliminate all forms of discrimination and violence against women working in public and private spaces (Khan, 2020). The program promotes income generation and improves women's income security while addressing structural barriers to women-owned SMEs. The initiative strengthens the capacity of women owner-managers of SMEs to work with the government in public and corporate procurement processes that aim to support women-owned SMEs.

5.6. Conclusion

This chapter addressed women entrepreneurs' crucial role in SMEs and advocated for better female representation in the information security and cybersecurity profession. The chapter discussed how women had broken the barrier into cybersecurity and information security careers. The following are key points that the chapter presents.

Key Points

- There are now more educated women entrepreneurs owning and managing SMEs with many now playing meaningful roles in supporting employment.
- Women are beginning to play an important role in ownership and management of SMEs globally.
- Despite the financial and technical challenges that women face when running SMEs, many are resilient and are self-reporting on efficacy to address these.

Chapter 6

Novel and Emergent Information and Cybersecurity Threats Facing SMEs during Lockdowns

6.1. Introduction

It is an open secret that many cyber criminals with nefarious intentions specifically target SMEs since these are perceived as more vulnerable due to adequate investment in the latest security defenses and tools (Benz & Chatterjee, 2020). Currently, many SMEs are witnessing what is generally termed a cyber-epidemic which is slowly gathering momentum post-Covid 19 pandemic-driven lockdowns. It is estimated that cybercrime may have costed businesses close to $ 6 trillion annually by the end of 2021, with global spending exceeding $1 trillion at the end of this date (Benz & Chatterjee, 2020). Studies by the National Small Business Association (NDBA) have shown that SMEs have been targets of attacks in over 50% of all cyberattack cases, with 43% explicitly targeting SMEs (Dent, 2021). Section 6.1 presents a discussion on the rise of new exploits that have targeted SMEs during COVID-19 lockdowns.

4IR technologies are set to disrupt the traditional way SMEs have been accustomed to managing information and cybersecurity threats. A 2018 study that measured the uniqueness of the cybersecurity attacks on businesses showed that in that year's second quarter, 32% of these attacks were considered unique and had not been witnessed before compared to the same quarter of the previous year (Benz & Chatterjee, 2020). SMEs are a constant source of attack by cybercriminals because of the opportunity to access money and information or by serving as points of escalated attacks on larger companies (Paulsen & Toth, 2016). Section 6.2 delves profoundly on the specialized cyberattacks that are bespoke to SMEs.

6.2. COVID-19 Pandemic Themed Exploits and Attacks to SMEs

The advent of the COVID-19 pandemic witnessed a surge in online activities when lockdowns were instituted globally to curb the spread of the virus. Computer activities increased as organizations shifted to adopting 'working from home' policies and creating the necessary networking infrastructure to enable this. During this period, to the present, communication technologies such as Zoom and Microsoft Teams were adopted and became very popular.

This was also the period cybercrime and cyberattacks were at their peak. The tried and tested phishing campaigns, and malicious email attachments were at their highest. Cybercriminals took advantage and exploited the anxieties of many, with many across the globe falling victims to targeted phishing campaigns.

6.2.1. Extended Phishing Campaigns

In Germany's North Rhine-Westphalia (NRW), cybercriminals created a fake website to solicit relief funds. Victims' personal unidentifiable information (PII) was harvested on these fake websites. The NRW officials reported that thousands of falsified requests were eventually granted. These falsified requests resulted in over $109 million being lost to cybercriminals. The TrickBot malware was primarily responsible for targeted phishing attacks and was distributed through emails that claimed to provide information regarding COVID-19 testing with no charge, with the actual intent being the harvesting of PII. Online 'forms' requesting PII were attached as links to these emails.

6.2.2. Emotet Malware

The Emotet Malware was a unique cyberattack targeted at the Rudolph and Stephanie Regional Hospital in Benešov, Czech Republic, at the peak of the COVID-19 pandemic (Kolouch, Zahradnický, & Kučínský, 2022). The severity was such that it paralyzed this institution for weeks, and those working at the hospital could not use X-rays, ultrasound, or laboratory instruments, nor were they able to exchange information with other hospitals. The cyberattack used a Trojan malware known as the Emotet Trojan, first identified by security researchers in 2014. The weakness of this small hospital was that its ICT security level was minimal (Kolouch et al., 2022). Although the Emotet Trojan was initially designed as banking malware, targeting financial institutions to gain unauthorized access to private data was tailored for this hospital attack. During this peak in the pandemic, scholars noted an increase in vulnerability to phishing attacks because many hospitals shifted many operations to remote working, putting weaknesses in security controls into sharp focus and negatively impeding hospital services.

6.2.3. Distributed Denial of Service (DDoS) Attack

A study carried out by Zhou, Gaurav, Gupta, Hamdi, and Nedjah (2021) shows that during the COVID-19 pandemic, there was a notable rise in distributed denial of service (DDoS) attacks. The nature of these attack types was that many compromised machines would generate voluminous packets of data directed at a target website server that would be overwhelmed, causing it to break down. According to Zhou et al. (2021), there was a 90% increase in DDos attacks in 2020 compared to the previous year due to the availability of many online tools. Examples of these tools are Trinoo, TFN2K, TFN, Mstream, Shaft, Knight, and many others, which were able to generate heavy attack traffic that would consequently restrict normal usage of websites. For SMEs, this was consequential as these restrictions adversely affected legitimate traffic. For example, the United States Department of Health and Human Services (HHS) faced several DDoS attacks from an unknown source. Hospitals in the Czech Republic, and France that were working on developing the COVID-19 vaccine, were also targeted. The acuteness of these attacks provoked a joint response by the UK's National Cyber Security Centre (NCSC) and USA's CISA. The findings were that the main targets were sensitive research from pharmaceutical companies, medical research organizations, and universities involved in COVID-19 (Lallie et al., 2021).

6.2.4. Bring Your Own Device (BYOD)

As personal computing devices such as smartphones and tablets grew smaller and smaller while their processing capabilities grew more extensive and complex, this led to more people performing work-related tasks with these devices, with many connecting these devices to the business network. Many businesses felt that bringing these devices into the workplace was pivotal to information security threats and posed significant risks. This practice of employees taking their computing devices to the workplace was coined 'bring your own device' or BYOD. As these intelligent devices proliferated, they would later pose a challenge to many businesses. Since businesses realized that it would be difficult to stop individuals from bringing these devices to the network and even more difficult to restrict them from connecting to the business network, policies were designed to manage and control BYOD to mitigate against security threats. At the onset of the COVID-19 pandemic, policies were challenged since employees would now be required to work from home, often with these same devices. It, therefore, required that businesses rethink better ways to protect the privacy of their own as well as the employee information and, importantly, the intellectual property of these businesses at home environments.

A study done by Scott, Mason, and Szewczyk (2021) that was concerned with the exposure of information held by inappropriately sanitized devices during the pandemic period sought to highlight the risks these devices posed, such as data breaches to businesses. A 'snapshot' analysis of BYOD policies businesses developed showed that most publicly available BYODs did not address information security risk issues. It was also unclear how businesses dealt with devices that reached their end of life or how they would be discarded, sold, or even stolen. Ali et al. (2020) points out that the COVID-19 pandemic triggered businesses to re-architect their traditional IT infrastructure. Businesses need to build a 'cyber confidence techno-centric architecture' as an 'alternate method of the work environment' for these business ecosystems to be driven remotely and enable BYOD.

6.3. More Specialized SME Attacks

The COVID-19 pandemic created unique opportunities for innovative cyber-attacks. At its peak, the pandemic forced most employees to work from home, many using their personal computers. Most SMEs were unprepared for the lockdown and failed to provide necessary off-site resources and support. Cybercriminals actively exploited this oversight for gain. The following sections discuss the more specialized cybercriminals' attacks during this period.

6.3.1. Ransomware Targeting SMEs

Ransomware attacks usually occur when malicious software infects a computer or a network by opening a link. This software is designed primarily to restrict access to essential data and information on a compromised computer and can encrypt files. The owner will only have access to these files when a ransom is paid. Richardson, North, and Garofalo (2021) reported that in mid-2022, there was an increase in losses caused by ransomware attacks and the cost of remediation. Because of the remediation's sensitivity and the ransom payment to attackers, many organizations were forced not only to pay but also to keep silent. A report by Coalition, a cyber-insurance provider, pointed out that ransomware accounted for 41% of all cyber insurance claims in 2021. As businesses and, in particular, SMEs begin to realize the value of information that this hold and how much they are willing to part with to retain this, cybercriminals have leveraged this to execute targeted attacks that restrict the use of the business's data for a ransom. The loss of such information, even temporarily, can have substantial financial implications for these SMEs. Cybercriminals have escalated attacks giving rise to ransomware attacks.

SMEs in the healthcare industries were the second most targeted organizations as these had fragile information security infrastructure when the COVID-19 pandemic was most prevalent. Some SMEs have been forced to pay ransoms to cybercriminals to prevent further catastrophes such as the loss of patient lives. Richardson et al. (2021) pointed out that most discovered malware was part of campaigns that targeted people searching for any visible website related to the COVID-19 pandemic and the coronavirus. For example, a research security team known as DomainTools discovered that people were downloading an Android application that would track the heatmap of COVID-19, only to realize that this was ransomware that would lock users' screens. For the users' screens to be enabled, they needed to pay a ransom (Richardson et al., 2021).

Bispham, Creese, Dutton, Esteve-Gonzalez, and Goldsmith (2021) reported an exceptionally severe ransomware attack on a German hospital, which exploited a 'directory traversal vulnerability that uses remote access technology. It is believed that this specific attack led to the death of a patient as the systems attacked were shut, and the patient could not get timely emergency attention and care. The case was later dropped since it was difficult to rule out that the death was not caused by server illness. This case demonstrates how severe ransomware attacks could be for vulnerable hospitals and SMEs.

6.3.2. Supply Chain Attacks Targeting SMEs

The COVID-19 pandemic drove the lockdown in early 2019. It allowed SMEs to reinvent business operations, with many relying on managed service providers (MSPs) as middlemen who would support remote access using collaboration tools. This infrastructure and arrangement proved very attractive for cybercriminals because when an MSP was compromised, the cybercriminal would potentially gain access to most of the SMEs and customers downstream. The cyberattacks were possible when SMEs and the MSPs configured the connectivity and remote access poorly, using vulnerable software, and not taking cognizance of secure remote access protocols. This process was more efficient than targeting the SME individually.

6.3.3. Attacks on Collaborative Tools

Video conference tools used by SMEs have been popular during the pandemic and lockdowns, with proportionally higher usage than any other recorded period. Such tools have been magnets for cybercriminals. These tools have solicited the attention of cybercriminals, who have assessed the weak points of these tools to execute targeted attacks. A tool such as Zoom was targeted with software vulnerability for this tool identified and being sold in dark-web markets. Zoom became a target of phishing attacks, with fake password-stealing meeting invitations being sent for these to harvest people's passwords. The cyberattack campaigns were and continue to be successful mainly because many SMEs are unfamiliar with the technologies and how these Zoom and other video conferencing technologies are used. Indeed, Microsoft Teams and users of the Cisco Webex did not escape these phishing attacks, and it was reported in their systems that certain 'notifications' would point users towards fake, credential-lifting login pages. As many as over 50,000 Microsoft 365 users were reported to have been victims of these phishing attacks. When the COVID-19 pandemic drove lockdowns in 2019, SMEs reinvented business operations, with many relying on managed service providers (MSPs) as middlemen who would support remote access using collaboration tools. This infrastructure and arrangement proved very attractive for cybercriminals because when an MSP was compromised, the cybercriminal would potentially gain access to most of the SMEs and customers downstream. The cyberattacks were possible when SMEs and the MSPs configured the connectivity and remote access poorly, using vulnerable software, and not taking cognizance of secure remote access protocols. This process was more efficient than targeting the SME individually.

6.3.4. Cross-Site Scripting (XSS)

At the peak of the Covid pandemic between periods 2019 and 2020, Cross-Site Scripting (XSS) was listed as one of the top ten vulnerabilities that appear on the Internet because many people were dependent on the Internet for operations (Wibowo & Sulaksono, 2021). XSS attacks typically occur when attackers inject dangerous and malicious software (malware), usually JavaScript, that targets a legitimate website (Wibowo & Sulaksono, 2021). This specific script is very dangerous, and an unwitting victim who has had their computers infected may cause damage to websites or be used by an attacker such as a hacker to control a user's web browser. Computers usually get infected when unsuspecting users click on links that lead to already compromised websites. Form infection, the XSS can then spread to other websites. XSS is most dangerous when combined with other attacks, such as Remote Code Execution (RCE) and Cross-Site Request Forgery (CSRF). During the pandemic, this led to high-level requirements for remote working using Remote Desktop Protocol (RDP). With users moving from RDP to personal devices within the same network and clicking on unauthorized links, XSS could quickly spread.

6.4. Conclusion

This chapter has addressed SMEs' novel and emergent information and cybersecurity threats. Emphasis was placed on novel information security threats occurring during the COVID-19 pandemic, which forced many to work from home. The following are key points that the chapter presents.

Key Points

- SMEs now face novel and emergent information and cybersecurity threats not witnessed before with many recorded incidents of new undocumented types of cyber-attacks.
- Novel attacks such as new versions of ransomware attacks, supply chain attacks are becoming popular forms of cyber-attacks to SMEs.
- Zoom and MS Teams video conferencing and collaborative tools used by SMEs to communicate with each other are possible vulnerable entry points used by cyber-criminals to launch targeted attacks to SMEs.

Chapter 7

Protecting Small Business Information in the Advent of Innovative Business Ideas

7.1. Introduction

Social philosophers such as Marx, Weber, Adorno, and Habermas considered developing business ideas through rationalization and human relations of the 'social man' (Nooteboom, 1988). The 'social man' concept provides context to emergent and new business management ideas. These philosophers shaped the current thinking on how SMEs would consider 'organizational humanism' and the need for harmony within businesses (Kao, Kao, & Kao, 2002). This chapter provides insights into the evolution of small business operations amidst the evolving technologies and innovative business ideas with focus on the Metaverse. Section 7.1 presents a background on the evolution of SMEs and the various management approaches and technology use. Section 7.2 presents new kinds of technology-centric SMEs of the future with emphasis on the Metaverse. The chapter concludes by the rising the implications of business models such as the Metaverse to the security of information in SMEs.

7.2. The Evolution of Small Business Management

Kao et al., (2002, p. 4) address how business and management ideas have evolved, shaping the thinking from market-driven economies to the current entrepreneurship as an alternative philosophy. The evolution of this thinking is shown in Table 6. The table shows a shift in thinking, where once, the financial benefit consumed business thinking, to the current entrepreneurial approach that has broadened the thinking to include wealth creation, and a value-adding process to society

The entrepreneurial approach that SMEs have primarily driven has presented new thoughts and ideas that have currently shaped how society now thinks about innovation and technology, which has become essential. When Charles Babbage patented the first mechanical calculator in 1822, this was the beginning of using calculating devices for business purposes (Kao et al., 2002). It was only until Alan Turing's innovations led to the development of large-scale electronic computing devices in 1944 that businesses realized the power of computing in business operations. These innovations and ideas have evolved to the current use of personal computing and the Internet, which have shaped the current SME environment. It may be argued that these changes did not necessarily improve the quality of management of business operations. Scholars note that since the 1940s;

> "There has been little or no progress in organization and business management to accompany the striking changes in the tools by which management practice is conducted." (Kao et al., 2002, p. 6)

Table 6. Information and Cybersecurity Issues for SMEs Use

Sequential Development	Management Thought	Proponents
Before the factory system of operation	Seeking harmony and the call for new moral order	Robert Owen (1771-1858)
Scientific management in operations	Scientific thinking in improving and reforming operations using facts	Fredrick Winslow Taylor (1856-1915)
Operational Efficiency	Performance and rewards/Bonus. Graphical aids	Carl Barth (1860-1939)
	Motion and Fatigue studies	Gantt (1861-1919)
	Efficiency through organization	Frank Bunker Gilberth (1868-1924) Lilian Bunker (1878-1972) Harrison Emerson (1853-1931)
The Human Factor	Industrial Psychology	Hugo Munsterberg (1863-1916)
The Social Man	Sociology in economics and Society	Vilfredo Pareto (1848-1923)
Administrative theory	Man and career development	Henri Fayol (1841-1925)
Union and management relations	Union–Management cooperation	Many
Entrepreneurship	Wealth creation by the individual to add societal value	Many including (Kao et al., 2002)

Source: Kao, Kao, & Kao (2002). Entrepreneurism: A philosophy and a sensible alternative for the market economy. World Scientific Publishing Company (p. 4).

7.3. New Kinds of Technology-Centric SMEs

The way SMEs operate is anticipated to change as the environment around them changes, and where change is happening so fast, no one can predict the future of small businesses. An explosion in software patents within the last 50 years has fueled the rise of powerful technology software and hardware hubs, siphoning and moving rich talent from region to region, impacting SMEs. The movement of talent brings about essential and long-lasting benefits to SMEs driving inventions in SMEs.

The evolution of new business models driven by new technology innovations can be seen through the history of how patents have increased year on year. For instance, Chattergoon and Kerr (2022) examined meticulously patents filed in the US Patent and Trademark Office from 1976 to 2020, focusing on new or improved valuable products. Their findings suggest that a considerable spike of software patents has been noticeable in recent years, as software began having widespread use.

SMEs competing for domination in the online consumer market may avoid costs by using less-expensive platforms and the Internet to crowdsource technology and software in order to remain competitive. Indeed, in the future, the location where the SME operates will not be seen as necessary because of advanced technologies. The introduction of technology such as the Metaverse will soon change the very idea of the traditional business model. Metaverse and the emergence of new ideas are discussed in the next section.

7.3.1. Metaverse and the Age of New Business Ideas for SMEs

The company is formally known as Facebook, and now Meta has pioneered the Metaverse, which is seen as developing a set of virtual spaces where users can create and explore with others who are not in the same physical space. This means physical and geographical proximities will be obsolete in the Metaverse space.

Businesses and users can virtually perform typical business operations traditionally reserved in the physical space. Through the prototype Metaverse, users can already hang out with friends, work, play, learn, shop, create, and more. This will have the potential to create entrepreneurial and interesting future ways of carrying out small business. The very idea of the Metaverse will not be limited to the possibilities known today but opens up the imagination to the future possibilities where augmented reality (AR) and virtual reality (VA) meet. Indeed, there are tremendous possibilities, such as working in a decentralized digital space where the use of cryptocurrency will flow unrestricted across the Metaverse. SMEs can utilize this technology to own up virtual spaces and currency, provide incredible value within this virtual world, and get remunerated in digital currencies. This model can be borrowed from the present-day decentralized social media platforms, which SMEs typically use to market their goods and services where SMEs can move from one platform to the next. The idea of gaming or creating physical business spaces or even imaginative ones in the Metaverse will grow similar to the gaming industry's creation of unimaginable virtual worlds and spaces.

According to Baltezarević, Baltezarević, and Baltezarević (2018), video gaming is expected to be a billion-dollar industry soon, with the growing demand for gaming opening up new industries and new business opportunities. Gaming will be part of the metaverse' new business models and innovations. As people spend billions of dollars in the virtual space and become more confident in interacting with each other virtually, the experience of such interactions will advance. These advancements will make people feel everything they are doing in the virtual environment, and these innovations will propel the gaming industry to explode in the Metaverse.

Weston (2022), in an article titled "5 Profitable Business Opportunities in Metaverse", provides a definition and context to the Metaverse. The Metaverse is considered as:

"a shared and persistent virtual space, which exists in real-time and emerges from the convergence of virtual reality and virtually enhanced physical reality." (Weston, 2022, p. 1)

Weston, (2022) lists five profitable opportunities that small businesses may explore in the device-independent Metaverse, namely;

- Immersive shopping experiences
- Immersive learning experiences
- Virtual events
- Social media
- Employee engagement

The Metaverse provides independence in business operations running on non-fungible tokens (NFTs) and digital currency. Many of the above business opportunities may be leveraged using technologies such as Augmented Reality (AR), the Internet of Things (IoT), unique technologies, and head-mounted gears. In the Metaverse, the web spaces will be virtual shared environments.

As a precursor to full business integration into the Metaverse and reaping the benefits of the next generation of Internet-driven e-Commerce, some small businesses have considered themselves metaverse companies. In contrast, others have started to develop metaverse platforms and push operations traditionally run-on silos into single shared virtual spaces.

To fully realize the benefits and opportunities in the Metaverse, SMEs could decentralize their operations by making some activities and tasks more collaborative and interoperable. This could help SMEs innovate newer digitally driven ideas such as placing innovative advertisement spaces, entertainment spaces, or even spaces to build games within games. SMEs may use new technologies such as non-fungible tokens (NFTs). In the Metaverse, everything will be connected and decentralized. SMEs and individual users may acquire and trade NFTs as they seek to provide value in the virtual world and get remunerated in NFTs. SMEs may also create virtual spaces such as virtual concerts, which can attract virtual users while watching with amazingly created virtual users such as comical characters such as superman or batman sitting next to a person. This may revolutionize the entertainment industry. As more people are attracted online, SMEs have more value and profitability.

An article published by *Fortune*, written by Quiroz-Gutierrez (2022) exemplifies the value and profitability of the Metaverse. The article presents what Sheikh Hamdan bin Mohammed bin Rashid al-Maktoum, crown prince of Dubai, calls a 'metaverse strategy' for Dubai that "will add 40,000 jobs and $4 billion to Dubai's economy in 5 years". Dubai aims to provide the necessary support in metaverse education targeted at the developer community, content creators, and users of digital platforms. Dubai's metaverse strategy will entail funding and support that fosters metaverse innovation and economic contribution. It is envisaged that a metaverse talent will be cultivated.

7.3.2. Protecting SMEs Information in the Metaverse

While there is excitement around the numerous possibilities and opportunities that the Metaverse presents, many SMEs still consider this an abstract concept, as many are yet to optimize on virtual reality, augmented reality, and blockchain. Moreover, SMEs are yet to consider or fully grasp the privacy and security issues that will emerge in the Metaverse. Considering that the Metaverse will, in principle, collect vast amounts of personal data, proper mechanisms are yet to be formulated on how confidential personal and biometric data such as physiological responses, facial expressions, vocal inflections, and vital signs will be kept and shared. As innovation around the Metaverse grows, regulatory developments for information protection will also grow in tandem. Regulatory frameworks for SMEs' proper collection, usage, transfer, and disposal of personal data drawn from the Metaverse will need to be developed. It is most likely that these regulations will need modification and revamping to ensure proper usage. Along with extensive growth opportunities, the Metaverse comes with legitimate concerns about privacy and data security.

Because the Metaverse is built around digital platforms, SMEs' immersion into the Metaverse may attract cyber criminals' intent on compromising SME platforms. Likely, the standard information security threats found through the Internet will replicate in the Metaverse arena. These threats would include immersed phishing attacks, where a user immersed in the Metaverse would encounter cyber criminals with nefarious motives. SMEs using the Metaverse may also face data hacking and attacks from malicious software tailored for the Metaverse. The complex architecture that the Metaverse will be built upon will bring unique and complex challenges presently unknown. Hackers may also target NFTs that will be commonly used in the Metaverse. Finally, the integrity of the identity of a company or user (the avatar) is critical in the Metaverse. If an attacker compromises on a user avatar for nefarious purposes, this may compromise the sustainability and pose an existential threat to the Metaverse model on interaction. SMEs will therefore be advised to invest in software and hardware that should preserve the integrity of interaction inside the Metaverse while ensuring user data privacy and protection. Trust will be a crucial component for the proper usage of the Metaverse. As the SMEs' adoption of the Metaverse gains traction in the foreseeable future, those managing these SMEs will have to be mindful of the regulatory environment governing user identity, trust, security, and privacy considerations.

7.4. Conclusion

This chapter has discussed how the Metaverse, the next frontier of social media use, interaction, and business model, could influence SMEs' information security posture. The following are key points that the chapter presents.

Key Points

- The Metaverse provides independence in business operations running on non-fungible tokens (NFTs) and digital currency.
- The Metaverse is a technology built around digital platforms encouraging social interaction, and SMEs' immersion into the Metaverse may attract cyber criminals' intent on compromising SME platforms.
- The Metaverse will shape how SMEs of the future manage information security.

Chapter 8

The Fourth Industrial Revolution and Information Security for SMEs

8.1. Introduction

The fourth industrial revolution (4IR) will fundamentally alter how SMEs operate (Serumaga-Zake & van der Poll, 2021). 4IR was initially coined by Klaus Schwab, founder and executive chairman of the World Economic Forum, in 2016 when articulating the unlimited possibilities of having billions of people connected using advanced mobile technology and moving between digital domains and offline realities (Kempen, 2019). According to Schwab (2017), the four main areas 4IR may impact SMEs include collaborative innovation, product enhancement, customer expectations, and organizational forms. It is now possible to use technology to change how SMEs manufacture goods, process services, and connect to consumers to improve the efficient delivery of products and services.

Much has been said about the benefits that 4IR technologies may present to SMEs, but it is crucial to address the contexts and challenges SMEs to face before such adoption. Of primary interest has been how SMEs may leverage these emergent technologies to make their processes and information these hold against advanced cyber threats and attacks. This chapter begins by elucidating the challenging environment SMEs face in light of 4IR technologies in the next section. Section 8.1 introduces the use of Artificial Intelligence and Machine learning as the preeminent technologies that can support Information Security initiatives in SMEs. Section 8.2 presents big data analytics and potential application in SMEs while Section 8.3 discusses how the Internet of Things (IoT) has impacted and further exacerbated information security challenges to SMEs.

8.2. Artificial Intelligence and Machine Learning in Information Security for SMEs

SMEs can leverage the benefits of advanced technologies in the fourth industrial revolution (4IR), such as artificial intelligence (AI) and machine learning, to train data sets that can help SMEs make good decisions. For software-driven SMEs, this approach is crucial and can enable SMEs to harness the computational power of deep learning. Large data sets for training algorithms are becoming cheaper and freely available across open systems, and innovative SMEs can use these sources to outperform the competition.

8.2.1. Artificial Intelligence and Machine Learning

The discipline of artificial intelligence (AI) can be considered a new science that applies to products and services by developing into new and intelligent products and services capable of increasing SMEs' efficiency. AI enables human-like intelligence and allows SMEs' customers to be better targeted and analyzed. Moreover, AI can identify customer behavior and discursive patterns. These intelligence products and services can mimic human intelligence and sometimes surpass it (Arzikulov, 2021). Machine learning (ML) allows algorithms developed within specific contexts to learn without being programmed. If managed well, these algorithms can be used by SMEs to complement and perform information and cybersecurity functions similarly to those information security practitioners or even better. Indeed, when ML is used in information and cybersecurity SME contexts, SMEs can be more competitive because the development costs of these algorithms are falling, and SMEs with the right know-how can access these algorithms at open-source platforms (Huang, Mezencev, McDonald, & Vannberg, 2017). ML can be applied to SMEs' data to identify patterns. The 'intelligence' embedded in these algorithms can assist SMEs in achieving better information and cybersecurity functions such as detecting viruses and malware in encrypted traffic, finding insider threats, as-well-as predicting nefarious online activities.

As previously suggested, SMEs can obtain cost-effective algorithms from open-source platforms. By obtaining these algorithms, SMEs can bridge the gap between the basic level of data and information that SMEs potentially hold and process to the more sophisticated information processing and analytics that have traditionally been the preserve of big businesses. This bridging the knowledge gap between SMEs and big businesses has arisen primarily because of access to open-source algorithms.

Table 7 below describes the possible information and cybersecurity issues that can be adopted for SMEs' use.

Table 7. Information and Cybersecurity Issues for SMEs Use

Information security issue	Use of AI and Machine Learning algorithms in Information Security	Possible to outsource this algorithms
Network threat identification	SMEs can use supervised or unsupervised learning algorithms to detects threats by constantly monitoring the behavior of the network for anomalies. Algorithms will process massive amounts of data in near real time to discover critical incidents.	Likely
Provide browser security when on the Internet	SMEs can use supervised or unsupervised learning algorithms to detect novel and emergent malware, viruses, Trojans, ransomware etc. Trying to hijack information systems endpoints based on patterns, attributes and behaviors.	Likely
Cloud security	SMEs can use supervised or unsupervised learning algorithms to protect operations through analyzing mistrustful cloud applications such as how users are logging in, and how user's location is unusual, from TCP/IP traffic analysis.	Most probably
Detecting any malicious software in TCI/IP network traffic	SMEs can use supervised or unsupervised learning algorithms to detect malicious software in TCP/IP network traffic by analyzing traffic data elements.	Likely

8.3. Big Data Analytics in SMEs: No Data Is Too Big for Small Businesses

For SMEs' intent on leveraging competitiveness, there are many benefits that big data analytics can offer. These benefits have previously not been considered possible and were seen as the preserve of big businesses. Indeed, big businesses have customarily enjoyed what is known as a first-mover advantage in appropriating the benefits of big data analytics to their organizations and adapting these new innovative technologies. Big businesses continue to benefit from big data analytics technologies is that these businesses are endowed with substantial financial resources, inevitably compelling SMEs to continue to play catch-up.

Nonetheless, SMEs may have the advantage of adapting more quickly to emergent technology changes such as big data analytics since these are less bureaucratic than big business. Furthermore, many SMEs can use data-derived solutions in bespoke ways that are very different from how big businesses carry on their operations Marr (2016). It can now be argued that big data should now not just be seen as a preserve for big businesses and that no data is too big for SMEs to derive potential advantage. With the increased free data accessible to big data technology platforms, the harnessing of the infinite value of big data by SMEs is now possible.

8.3.1. Improving Analytic Capabilities of SMEs

SMEs can improve in-house analytics capabilities by moving from the traditional approach of manually collecting data and performing basic analytics to more advanced approaches. The approach to advanced analytic capabilities is possible if algorithms can be used to determine or predict what went wrong in the production process to predictive and prescriptive analytics capabilities. While it is possible to dismiss some of these suggestions as utopia, particularly for SMEs, there are already examples of predictive analytics in use by SMEs in developing economies to improve operations performance and create sustainable competitive advantages (Akpan, Udoh, & Adebisi, 2020).

SMEs using predictive analytics capabilities will utilize AI to predict, for example, if a production part will be faulty if customers would be interested in a specific product, or how much customers are willing to pay for a particular product or service. SMEs may need assistance in obtaining the skills necessary to train algorithms that apply to those variables and harvesting as much data concerning those variables as much as possible. Having leveraged these AI systems, SMEs can reduce costs and increase productivity.

8.3.2. Big Data Use for Information Security by SMEs

As SMEs digitize their operations and transact online, data created from these transactions, stored, modified, and even archived has become an extremely valued asset to these SMEs. Collectively, SMEs generate large volumes of data, and any person who knows how to analyze 'big data' will ultimately have a greater advantage. Industrious SMEs that are proactive in appropriating the benefit of big data analytics will be able to understand their customers better and serve their needs better, resulting in satisfied customers (Björkman & Franco, 2017).

Considering big data from the Volume, Velocity, and Variety (3Vs) will go beyond SMEs' capacity to store, process, and analyze such extensive data. While big business has such capabilities, SMEs have lagged. One possible reason that SMEs lag behind is that capacity and resources to leverage the potential use of huge volumes and other data sources is lacking. SMEs can increase their knowledge regarding big data analytics and the underlying concepts by disregarding the assumption that big data is too big for them to comprehend, let alone harness to their advantage (Iqbal, Kazmi, Manzoor, Soomrani, Butt & Shaikh, 2018).

8.3.3. Security Threat Analysis in SMEs Using Big Data

Security threat analysis can be leveraged using big data analytics, providing SMEs with actionable insights needed to drive business growth (Polkowski et al., 2017). SMEs can use information obtained from big data analytics for risk assessment based on large data sets such as media access control (MAC) addresses of computers that are active across the internet, Internet protocol (IP), and the location of these computers. Analytics on meta-data, devoid of personal information, such as where the SMEs products are popular and who is interested, and the duration of interest of a product or service on an SME's website can be collected. Actionable insights can also be collected about cybercriminals' behavior patterns, such as the kinds of targets that are more popular, the modus operandi of attacks, and the tools used in the attack (Krishnappa, 2015).

Auspiciously, newer and easily available open-source technology platforms that enable big data analytics solutions are readily available for SMEs to explore. What is changing is that soon, the term ''big data'' will be an abstract term because big data will no longer be a term tied to the size of a business. Furthermore, many data processing platforms harness volume, variety, and velocity beyond their ability to store and process and become cloud-based such as infrastructure-as-a-service (IaaS) (Rusaneanu & Lavric, 2014). These open platforms will enable SMEs to determine business strategies while opening up avenues where strategies align with big data analytics adoption (Wang, Yang, Pathan, Salam, Shahzad, & Zeng, 2018). It will be possible for SMEs to extract more accurate information from big data analytics while moving away from the traditional approach where only small data sets determine the strategy that they were previously accustomed to (Shah et al., 2017).

8.3.4. Examples of Open Source Platforms for Security Threat Analysis in SMEs

SMEs can benefit from the following three big data analytics platforms that are discussed: namely Google Analytics, Cognos Analytics, InsightSquared, and Sales Manago. Some of these are free and open-source, and some may require some financial investments to optimally leverage their usefulness.

Google Analytics is a freely available open and cloud-based platform that can be useful to SMEs with a web presence intending to extract long-term data about their operations. Google Analytics Software as a Service (SaaS) platform can assist SMEs in drawing accurate data-driven decision-making through free access to complex databases which show and track SMEs' customers' inbound traffic and how long the customers spend time interacting with SME products and services (Liu et al., 2020). IBM's Cognos Analytics is an equally helpful tool the SMEs can draw valuable business intelligence insights (Armenia, Angelini, Nonino, Palombi, & Schlitzer). Cognos Analytics offers a simple and accessible user-interface platform that provides valuable data solutions. InsightSquared is also a free tool that generates visual sales reports, and this can assist SMEs with accurate decisions about customers' preferences allowing for improved sales. InsightSquared also enables SMEs to discover new trends in customer data. Its value can be leveraged further by its inbuilt ability to connect to other tools, such as Google Analytics. Another tool that can benefit SMEs with big data analytics is Sales Manago, which is used in Poland to help SMEs automate their marketing services. Sales Manago can monitor 90 large volumes of emails and dynamic content on websites (Polkowski et al., 2017).

Insights into such large amounts of freely available data to SMEs is invaluable, and it is expected that the more proactive and innovative tech-savvy SMEs will make better decisions using such opportunities. It is argued that this is the appropriate time for SMEs to adopt big data analytics across their business operation in the era of 4IR (Marr, 2016). SMEs must overcome the perception barrier because tools are now openly available (Motau & Kalema, 2016; Sen, Ozturk & Vayvay, 2016).

The dividends are rewarding for the SMEs brave enough to overcome this perception barrier. Big data analytics could lead to significant improvements in business performance for SMEs with entrepreneurial tendencies and the ability to adapt swiftly to new changes. While the advantages of big data analytics may seem straightforward, some studies still show that SMEs are less likely to adopt it in their business activities (Sen et al., 2016; Leboea, 2017).

Table 8. Dimensions of Information Security

Organization culture	External Factors	Cognition	Security Factors	Fear of Technology	Lack or resources
Lack of data capturing and documentation	Competition pressure (existence of cases or examples)	Lack of knowledge	Lack of trust	Fear of trying new things	Lack of financial resources
Lack of data management (quality)	Government polices and laws	Not knowing how	Open resources regulation	Previous technology experience	Lack of skills
Intuition decision making	Vendor and big companies support	Ignorance	Risk	Complexity tolerance	Lack of technical capability
Leadership style (Open person runs the whole organization)	IT infrastructure	Informatization level in the country	Level of IT knowledge	Deployment of big data in the industry	Data resources
Lack of flexibility and resistance to change	Environmental pressure	Paradigm shift		IT and business alignment	

SMEs should address the concerns that hold them back from deriving the full benefits of big data analytics. Questions such as readiness, having the right people to drive the process, where to obtain the right tools and technologies and who will continuously monitor the big data analytic process are relevant questions that SME owner-managers must address. The Table 8 above presents six dimensions: Organization culture, External Factors, Cognition, Security Factors, Fear of Technology, and Lack of resources; each factor will be briefly discussed below.

8.4. The Internet of Everything and Impact to Information Security in SMEs

The Internet of Everything (IoE) considers the bigger picture of the Internet of Things (IoT). It considers the realm where the physical and cyberspace meet, with cyberspace permeating offline spaces and blurring the material and virtual worlds (DeNardis, 2020). According to Snyder & Byrd (2017), the key to the evolution of IoE has been the maturing fields of Artificial Intelligence, machine learning, and cognitive computing. The maturing of these technologies has enabled IoT systems to become IoE systems.

IoE was coined by Cisco, a leading company in network security and technologies for human computer interaction (Miraz, Ali, Excell, & Picking, 2015). Miraz et al. (2015) has pointed out that;

> "IoE has the potential to extract and analyse real-time data from the millions of sensors connected to it and then to apply it to aid automated and people-based processes." (Miraz et al., 2015, p. 220)

As IoE continues to be deployed across global and connected information software and hardware systems, it is paramount to understand 'what' and 'why' of the security and privacy design of IoE (Mohanty, 2020).

8.5. Conclusion

This chapter has examined and elaborated on the possible fourth industrial revolution (4IR) technologies SMEs could use to make their operations efficient. These technologies include artificial intelligence, machine learning, big data, and the Internet of Things. The following are key points that the chapter presents.

Key Points

- SMEs capable of using 4IR technologies such as AI and machine learning to their advantage.
- AI and Machine learning costs are falling, making these accessible to SMEs.

- 4IR technologies such as AI, machine learning, big data and Internet of Things (IoT) is changing the nature of how businesses operate.
- The application of big data to SMEs suggests that no data is too big for small businesses and those SMEs can benefit from big data analytics in a similar manner to big businesses.
- There are various free open-source platforms accessible to SMEs for big data analytics.

Chapter 9

Synopsis to Information Security in SMEs and the Future of Technology

9.1. Synopsis on Information Systems Security

In Chapter 1, the book articulated why SMEs need to consider embedding information and cybersecurity practices in their businesses. Already there is evidence that SMEs are beginning to take note of the emerging technology threats resulting from the increased use of technology. Chapter 1 explains that new socio-structural systems are emerging in the backdrop of business process improvement and technology transformation. Chapter 1 also alludes to the critical role SMEs play in many economies, the contributions these make to poverty alleviation and increasing employment opportunities for many, and importantly, the positive impact these make on increasing the GDPs of many economies. The importance of why SMEs should be protected and supported from cybersecurity threats was emphasized. The stability of SMEs is crucial as many experience challenges competing, and the nature of the challenges requires that owner-managers re-think their information and cybersecurity approaches.

9.2. Synopsis on the Disciplines of Information Systems Security and Cybersecurity

In Chapter 2, the contribution that the two fields of information security and cybersecurity are brought to the fore. These two fields show how SMEs' data, information, and technology should be protected from various perspectives and concerns. However, they may seem similar—chapter 2 points to their distinct differences. SMEs may learn and draw on valuable insights. As Chapter 2 explains, many SMEs struggle to protect their systems from outsiders, such as hackers with nefarious intentions. SMEs have been seen as weak or soft targets since many owner-managers do not invest significantly in information and cybersecurity protection. The argument presented in Chapter 2 is that SMEs can be proactive by taking measures to protect themselves. Chapter 2 postulates that when SMEs apply these measures in wholesome to their local contexts, SMEs are the better defense against a wide range of threats. Chapter 2 concluded by suggesting that attitudes influenced by the level of education and technical know-how can adversely impede these measures. It is suggested then that SMEs use efficiently and freely available tools that can add insights into their management of information and cybersecurity threats. Tips on how better SMEs can protect themselves, the available standard control tools, and benchmarks against best practices are presented.

9.3. Synopsis on Technology Evolution

Chapter 3 points to SMEs operating under the ear of 4IR with the many possible opportunities to adopt and become innovative and competitive. While Chapter 3 unpacks the historical development of technology and how this has shaped the competitive business space, this chapter also unpacks the kinds and types of innovative technologies that characterize 4IR technologies such as 5G, IoT, big data, AI, and machine learning. Chapter 3 explains how these technologies have presented opportunities and, at the same time, challenges for SMEs because of the embedded these risks carry to SMEs not sufficiently knowledgeable in using these to leverage their competitiveness. Chapter 3 points out the accelerated use of these technologies, particularly during the COVID-19 pandemic when most employees were required to work from home because of lockdowns. There was a record number of cyber-crimes reported during this period targeting SMEs. Chapter 3 addressed the importance of technology evolution in hardware and software and how these have been applied against SMEs. A discourse on what can be done by owner-managers is provided, and a proposed information security governance approach is given.

9.4. Synopsis of Information Systems Security Behavior and Culture

In Chapter 4, the behavior and culture of those managing SMEs are examined. Chapter 4 explains that behavior has influenced how SMEs to address information and cybersecurity risk providing essential pointers to how negative behavior, culture, and habits exacerbate the security risk posture of SMEs. It is shown that the behavior will determine how SMEs will decide on the types and kinds of information technologies to use and how these will be used. Chapter 4 also addresses the critical consideration SME owner-managers should take on the role their own employees (called insiders) play regarding information security threats. This chapter points to insiders posing more of an information security threat than expected and offers guidance on how SMEs may protect themselves against insiders. Chapter 4 shows how SMEs may inculcate positive behavior amongst their employees while fostering better information and cybersecurity management principles. Various frameworks on how this can be done are offered, and importantly, how employees can be co-creators of a better information security culture within their SMEs.

9.5. Synopsis of Information Systems Security and the Role of Women Entrepreneurs

Chapter 5 addressed an under-considered theme in the context of SMEs, namely that women are beginning to play an essential role in the ownership and management of SMEs globally. Chapter 5 points to the technical and financial struggles women face in managing SMEs and highlight how such struggles effectively influence their ability to address information and cybersecurity concerns. This chapter explains that women have been playing a more meaningful role in information and cybersecurity than previously with many young educated women. The young women self-report their efficacy in dealing with information and cybersecurity challenges in equal to even better proportion than men.

9.6. Synopsis of Novel and Emergent Information and Cybersecurity Threats

In Chapter 6, the notion that SMEs now face novel and emergent information and cybersecurity threats are presented. Now, new undocumented types of cyber-attacks have changed how information and cybersecurity are managed. Chapter 6 discusses how these new attacks have increased in the advent of the COVID-19 pandemic costing trillions of dollars of business losses. New kinds of novel attacks, such as new versions of ransomware and supply chain attacks, are discussed in this chapter and are the more popular attacks targeting SMEs by cybercriminals. Chapter 6 also presents Zoom and MS Teams video conferencing and collaborative tools used by SMEs to communicate with each other as possible vulnerable entry points used by cyber-criminals to launch targeted attacks on SMEs. The possible usefulness of AI in various information and cybersecurity management areas is presented in tabular format in Chapter 4.

9.7. Synopsis of Protecting Small Business Information in the Advent of Innovative Business Ideas

In Chapter 7, business philosophy is discussed in the context of new and future innovation. The evolution of how small businesses evolved and what the future lies ahead for these businesses was presented. The focus was given to the Metaverse and a new and emerging technology that will shape not only the present business model of SMEs but also the information and cybersecurity challenges ahead. The chapter addressed how future SMEs should take cognizance of opportunities and challenges present in the Metaverse but proposes guidelines on how to adapt to these technologies safely.

9.8. Synopsis of the Fourth Industrial Revolution and Information Security

In Chapter 8, 4IR technologies are discussed, and their importance to SMEs is addressed. The Chapter begins by explaining how these technologies have influenced the competitiveness of SMEs and how innovative SMEs can leverage competitiveness by making these technologies part of their daily operations. The Chapter draws on significant concerns suggested by Serumaga-Zake and van der Poll (2021) on how 4IR has altered businesses. Chapter 7 unpacks the four areas of 4IR: collaborative innovation, product enhancement, customer expectations, and organizational forms as forms of 4IR innovativeness that can, if properly harnessed, change the future of how SMEs operate. The importance of Artificial intelligence (AI) to SMEs is considered taking cognizance that SMEs often shy away from harnessing the power of AI with misplaced perceptions that they are not tech-savvy enough for these advancements. Discussions on the usefulness of AI in the SME context are raised primarily when the costs of AI and machine learning is falling. Chapter 8 also points to the use of big data by SMEs and raises an important consideration that no data is too big for small businesses and that SMEs can similarly benefit from big data analytics to big businesses. How SMEs can improve their analytic capabilities is presented, and areas where bid data can be applied to manage information and cybersecurity challenges are presented. Chapter 8 points to the various open-source platforms SMEs can adopt for information security initiatives (Liu, 2014). Examples of these platforms are provided.

About the Author

Kennedy Njenga
College of Business and Economics,
Department of Applied Information Systems
University of Johannesburg, South Africa

Prof. Kennedy Njenga received his Ph.D. from the University of Cape Town, South Africa, in 2009 and has recently completed an Executive Education program at Harvard Business School. He is currently an Associate Professor at the Department of Applied Information Systems, the University of Johannesburg in South Africa. He has published and presented his research nationally and internationally in the information systems and technology field. His research focuses on methodological, philosophical, and behavioral issues related to privacy, security, and data protection held by technology systems. He also has a particular research interest in behavior and protecting technology around the Internet of Things (IoT), cloud computing, and big data. His work has been published in outlets such as the European Journal of Information Systems (EJIS), the Interdisciplinary Journal of Information, Knowledge, and Management (IJIKM), the African Journal of Information Systems (AJIS), and proceedings such as the Pacific Asian Conference on Information Systems (PACIS).

References

Acs, Z. J., & Preston, L. (1997). Small and medium-sized enterprises, technology, and globalization: Introduction to a special issue on small and medium-sized enterprises in the global economy. *Small Business Economics*, 9(1), 1-6.

Afolayan, A. O., & de la Harpe, A. C. (2020). The role of evaluation in SMMEs' strategic decision-making on new technology adoption. *Technology Analysis & Strategic Management*, 32(6), 697-710.

Akpan, I. J., Udoh, E. A. P., & Adebisi, B. (2020). Small business awareness and adoption of state-of-the-art technologies in emerging and developing markets, and lessons from the COVID-19 pandemic. *Journal of Small Business & Entrepreneurship*, 1-18. 92

Al Hogail, A. (2015). Cultivating and assessing an organizational information security culture ; an empirical study. *International Journal of Security and Its Applications*, 9(7), 163-178.

Al Hogail, A., & Mirza, A. (2014). A proposal of an organizational information security culture framework. Paper presented at the Proceedings of International Conference on Information, *Communication Technology and System* (ICTS) 2014.

Ali, M. I., Kaur, S., Khamparia, A., Gupta, D., Kumar, S., Khanna, A., & AlTurjman, F. (2020). Security challenges and cyber forensic ecosystem in IOT driven BYOD environment. *IEEE Access*, 8, 172770-172782.

Anwar, M., He, W., Ash, I., Yuan, X., Li, L., & Xu, L. (2017). Gender difference and employees' cybersecurity behaviors. *Computers in Human Behavior*, 69, 437-443.

Armenia, S., Angelini, M., Nonino, F., Palombi, G., & Schlitzer, M. F. (2021). A dynamic simulation approach to support the evaluation of cyber risks and security investments in SMEs. *Decision Support Systems*, 113580.

Arzikulov, O. (2021). Artificial intelligence to increase the efficiency of small businesses. *ISJ Theoretical & Applied Science*, 08 (100), 412-415.

Aterido, R., Beck, T., & Iacovone, L. (2013). Access to finance in Sub-Saharan Africa: is there a gender gap ? *World development*, 47, 102-120.

Auyporn, W., Piromsopa, K., & Chaiyawat, T. (2020). Critical Factors in Cybersecurity for SMEs in Technological Innovation Era. Paper presented at the *ISPIM Conference Proceedings*.

Avery, J. S. (2012). *Information theory and evolution*. Singapore: World Scientific Publishing Company.

Baltezarević, R., Baltezarević, B., & Baltezarević, V. (2018). The video gaming industry: From play to revenue. *International Review* (3-4), 71-76.

Barton, K. A., Tejay, G., Lane, M., & Terrell, S. (2016). Information system security commitment: A study of external influences on senior management. *Computers & security*, 59, 9-25.

Baskerville, R. (1993). Information systems security design methods: implications for information systems development. *ACM Computing Surveys (CSUR)*, 25(4), 375-414.

References

Baracaldo, N., & Joshi, J. (2013). An adaptive risk management and access control framework to mitigate insider threats. *Computers & security*, 39, 237-254.

Bell, S. (2017). Cybersecurity is not just a'big business' issue. *Governance Directions*, 69(9), 536-539.

Benz, M., & Chatterjee, D. (2020). Calculated risk? A cybersecurity evaluation tool for SMEs. *Business Horizons*, 63(4), 531-540.

Beyer, S., Rynes, K., & Haller, S. (2004). Deterrents to women taking computer science courses. *IEEE technology and society magazine*, 23(1), 21-28.

Bhattacharya, D. (2013). Evolution of information security issues in small businesses. Paper presented at the *Journal of the Colloquium for Information Systems Security Education*.

Bispham, M., Creese, S., Dutton, W. H., Esteve-Gonzalez, P., & Goldsmith, M. (2021). *Cybersecurity in Working from Home: An Exploratory Study*. TPRC49: The 49th Research Conference on Communication, Information and Internet Policy, Available at SSRN: http://dx.doi.org/10.2139/ssrn.3897380

Björkman, F., & Franco, S. (2017). *How big data analytics affect decisionmaking: A study of the newspaper industry*. Master's Thesis. Uppsala University.

Bonneau, J., Herley, C., Van Oorschot, P. C., & Stajano, F. (2015). Passwords and the evolution of imperfect authentication. *Communications of the ACM*, 58(7), 78-87.

Bueechl, J., Haerting, R., Pressl, M., & Kaim, R. (2021). Potentials and Barriers of Agility in Small and Medi-um Sized Enterprises: Insights From Qualitative Research in Germany. Paper presented at the *Business Information Systems*.

Buil-Gil, D., Miró-Llinares, F., Moneva, A., Kemp, S., & Díaz-Castaño, N. (2021). Cybercrime and shifts in opportunities during COVID-19: a preliminary analysis in the UK. *European Societies*, 23(sup1), S47-S59.

Bulgurcu, B., Cavusoglu, H., & Benbasat, I. (2010). Information security policy compliance: an empirical study of rationality-based beliefs and information security awareness. *MIS quarterly*, 523-548. 17

Chattergoon, B., & Kerr, W. R. (2022). Winner takes all ? Tech clusters, population centers, and the spatial transformation of US invention. *Research Policy*, 51(2), 104418.

Chatterjee, D. (2019). Should executives go to jail over cybersecurity breaches? *Journal of Organizational Computing and Electronic Commerce*, 29(1), 1-3.

Chen, Y., Galletta, D. F., Lowry, P. B., Luo, X., Moody, G. D., & Willison, R. (2021). Understanding Inconsistent Employee Compliance with Information Security Policies Through the Lens of the Extended Parallel Process Model. *Information systems research*. 32(3):1043-1065.

Copeland, J. (2012). *Alan Turing: The codebreaker who saved 'millions of lives'*. Retrieved from https://www.bbc.com/news/technology-18419691.

Cybersecurity-Guide. (2021). *A guide for women in cybersecurity*. Retrieved from https://cybersecurityguide.org/resources/women-in-cybersecurity/

Dent, P. A. (2021). *Cybersecurity Failures of Small and Medium-Sized Businesses: Circumventing Leadership Failure*. Utica: Utica College.

DeNardis, L. (2020). *The Internet in everything*. New Haven: Yale University Press.

References

Din, Z., Jambari, D. I., Yusof, M. M., & Yahaya, J. (2020). Information Systems Security Management for Internet of Things: Enabled Smart Cities Conceptual Framework. Paper presented at the *SMARTGREENS*.

Dini, G., & Lopriore, L. (2015). Password systems: Design and implementation. *Computers & Electrical Engineering*, 47, 318-326.

Emer, A., Unterhofer, M., & Rauch, E. (2021). A Cybersecurity Assessment Model for Small and Medium-Sized Enterprises. *IEEE Engineering Management Review*.

Erasmus, L., Reynolds, A., & Fourie, H. (2019). A generic balanced scorecard for small and medium manufacturing enterprises in South Africa. *The Southern African Journal of Entrepreneurship and Small Business Management*, 11(1), 1-15.

Friedman, H. H., Friedman, L. W., & Leverton, C. (2016). Increase diversity to boost creativity and enhance problem solving. *Psychosociological Issues in Human Resource Management*, 4(2), 7.

Georgiadou, A., Mouzakitis, S., & Askounis, D. (2021). Designing a cybersecurity culture assessment survey targeting critical infrastructures during COVID-19 crisis. *International Journal of Network Security & Its Applications (IJNSA)* Vol, 13.

Georgiadou, A., Mouzakitis, S., & Askounis, D. (2021). Detecting Insider Threat via a Cyber-Security Culture Framework. *Journal of Computer Information Systems*, 1-11.

Gilovich, T., Medvec, V. H., & Chen, S. (1995). Commission, omission, and dissonance reduction: Coping with regret in the "Monty Hall" problem. *Personality and Social Psychology Bulletin*, 21(2), 182- 190.

Govender, N. M., & Pretorius, M. (2015). A critical analysis of information and communications technology adoption: The strategy-aspractice perspective. *Acta Commercii*, 15(1), 1-13.

Govender, S. G., Kritzinger, E., & Loock, M. (2020). A Framework for the Assessment of Information Security Risk, the Reduction of 55 Information Security Cost and the Sustainability of Information Security Culture. Paper presented at *the Computer Science On-line Conference*.

Gupta, A., & Hammond, R. (2005). Information systems security issues and decisions for small businesses: An empirical examination. *Information Management & Computer Security*. 13(4), 297-310. https://doi.org/10.1108/09685220510614425

Hansen, E. B., & Bøgh, S. (2021). Artificial intelligence and internet of things in small and medium-sized enterprises: A survey. *Journal of Manufacturing Systems*, 58, 362-372.

Hansen, H., & Rand, J. (2014). Estimates of gender differences in firm's access to credit in Sub-Saharan Africa. *Economics Letters*, 123(3), 374-377.

Hoffman, S. F., & Friedman, H. H. (2018). Machine Learning and Meaningful Careers: Increasing the Number of Women in STEM. *Journal of Research in Gender Studies*, 8(1), 11-27.

Huang, C., Mezencev, R., McDonald, J. F., & Vannberg, F. (2017). Open source machine-learning algorithms for the prediction of optimal cancer drug therapies. *PLoS One*, 12(10), e0186906.

Humaidi, N., & Balakrishnan, V. (2015). Leadership styles and information security compliance behavior: The mediator effect of information security awareness. *International Journal of Information and Education Technology*, 5(4), 311.

References

International LabourConference. (2015). *Small and medium-sized enterprises and decent and productive employment creation.* Retrieved from Geneva: https://www.ilo.org/wcmsp5/groups/public/---ed_norm/---relconf/documents/meetingdocument/wcms_358294.pdf

Kankanhalli, A., Teo, H.-H., Tan, B. C., & Wei, K.-K. (2003). An integrative study of information systems security effectiveness. *International journal of information management,* 23(2), 139-154.

Kao, R. R., Kao, K. R., & Kao, R. W. (2002). *Entrepreneurism: A philosophy and a sensible alternative for the market economy.* Singapore: World Scientific Publishing Company.

Kempen, A. (2019). The 4th Industrial Revolution-hidden threats to human and cybersecurity? *Servamus Community-based Safety and Security Magazine,* 112(10), 10-12.

Khan, M. K. (2020). Overcoming Gender Disparity in Cybersecurity Profession. Retrieved from https://www.g20-insights.org/policy_briefs/overcoming-gender-disparity-in-cybersecurity-profession/

Ključnikov, A., Mura, L., & Sklenár, D. (2019). Information security management in SMEs: factors of success. *Entrepreneurship and Sustainability Issues,* 6(4), 2081.

Kolouch, J., Zahradnický, T., & Kučínský, A. (2022). Ransomware Attacks on Czech Hospitals at Beginning of COVID-19 Crisis. In: Tušer, I., Hošková-Mayerová, Š. (eds) *Trends and Future Directions in Security and Emergency Management.* Lecture Notes in Networks and Systems, vol 257. Springer, Cham. https://doi.org/10.1007/978-3-030-88907-4_18

Kumar, R., Singh, R. K., & Dwivedi, Y. K. (2020). Application of industry 4.0 technologies in SMEs for ethical and sustainable operations: Analysis of challenges. *Journal of cleaner production,* (1)275:124063.

Lallie, H. S., Shepherd, L. A., Nurse, J. R., Erola, A., Epiphaniou, G., Maple, C., & Bellekens, X. (2021). Cyber security in the age of COVID-19: A timeline and analysis of cyber-crime and cyber-attacks during the pandemic. *Computers & security,* 105, 102248.

Leboea, S. (2017). The factors influencing SME failure in South Africa (online). MBA, University of Cape Town. Retrieved from https://open.uct.ac.za/handle/11427/25334

Liu, C. (2014). The enemy within: the inherent security risks of temporary staff. *Computer Fraud & Security,* 2014(5), 5-7.

Lloyd, G. (2020). The business benefits of cyber security for SMEs. *Computer Fraud & Security,* 2020(2), 14-17.

Lowry, P. B., Posey, C., Roberts, T. L., & Bennett, R. J. (2014). Is your banker leaking your personal information ? The roles of ethics and individual-level cultural characteristics in predicting organizational computer abuse. *Journal of Business Ethics,* 121(3), 385-401.

Lowry, P. B., Posey, C., Bennett, R. J., & Roberts, T. L. (2015). Leveraging fairness and reactance theories to deter reactive computer abuse following enhanced organisational information security policies: An empirical study of the influence of counterfactual reasoning and organisational trust. *Information Systems Journal,* 25(3), 193- 273.

Lundgren, B., & Möller, N. (2019). Defining information security. *Science and engineering ethics*, 25(2), 419-441.

Luthra, S., & Mangla, S. K. (2018). Evaluating challenges to Industry 4.0 initiatives for supply chain sustainability in emerging economies. *Process Safety and Environmental Protection*, 117, 168-179.

Markovic, S., Koporcic, N., Arslanagic-Kalajdzic, M., Kadic-Maglajlic, S., Bagherzadeh, M., & Islam, N. (2021). Business-to-business open innovation: COVID-19 lessons for small and medium-sized enterprises from emerging markets. *Technological Forecasting and Social Change*, 170, 120883.

Marr, B. (2016). *Big Data for small business for dummies*. West Sussex: John Wiley & Sons.

McCumber, J. (1991). Information systems security: A comprehensive model. Paper presented at the *Proceedings 14th National Computer Security Conference*.

Miraz, M. H., Ali, M., Excell, P. S., & Picking, R. (2015). A review on Internet of Things (IoT), Internet of everything (IoE) and Internet of nano things (IoNT). *2015 Internet Technologies and Applications (ITA)*, 219-224.

Mohanty, S. P. (2020). Security and Privacy by Design is Key in the Internet of Everything (IoE) Era. *IEEE Consumer Electron. Mag.*, 9(2), 4-5.

Morgan, S. (2019). *Women Represent 20 Percent Of The Global Cybersecurity Workforce In 2019*. Retrieved from https://cybersecurityventures.com/women-in-cybersecurity-20-percent-2019/

Morris, M. G., Venkatesh, V., & Ackerman, P. L. (2005). Gender and age differences in employee decisions about new technology: An extension to the theory of planned behavior. *IEEE transactions on engineering management*, 52(1), 69-84. 70

Müller, J. M., Buliga, O., & Voigt, K. I. (2018). Fortune favors the prepared: How SMEs approach business model innovations in Industry 4.0. *Technological Forecasting and Social Change*, 132, 2-17.

Muthuppalaniappan, M., & Stevenson, K. (2021). Healthcare cyber-attacks and the COVID-19 pandemic: an urgent threat to global health. *International Journal for Quality in Health Care*, 33(1), mzaa117.

Nazareth, D. L., & Choi, J. (2015). A system dynamics model for information security management. *Information & Management*, 52(1), 123-134.

Ncubukezi, T., Mwansa, L., & Rocaries, F. (2020). A Proposed: Integration of the Monte Carlo model and the Bayes network to Propose Cyber Security Risk Assessment Tool for Small and Medium Enterprises in South Africa. *IJISRT*, 3(18), 152-155.

Nel, F., & Drevin, L. (2019). Key elements of an information security culture in organisations. *Information & Computer Security*, (27)2, 146-164. https://doi.org/10.1108/ICS-12-2016-0095

Nilles, J. M. (1976). *Telecommunications-transportation tradeoff: Options for tomorrow*: New York ; John Wiley & Sons, Inc.

Nooteboom, B. (1988). The Facts About Small Business and the Real Values of Its 'Life World': A Social Philosophical Interpretation of This Sector of the Modem Economy. *American journal of economics and sociology*, 47(3), 299-314.

References

Onyejekwe, C.J. (2011). Internet: empowering women? *Pakistan Journal of Women's Studies: Alam-e-Niswan*, 18(2), 53-63 Retrieved from https://www.thefreelibrary.com/The+internet%3a+empowering+women%3f-a0346627614

Paganini, L., & Gama, K. (2020). Female participation in hackathons: A case study about gender issues in application development marathons. *IEEE Revista Iberoamericana de Tecnologias del Aprendizaje*, 15(4), 326-335.

Paulsen, C., & Toth, P. (2016). *Small business information security*. US Department of Commerce. https://doi.org/10.6028/NIST.IR.7621r1

Phelps, B. E. (1980). Early Electronic Computing Developments at IBM. *Annals of the History of Computing*, 2(3), 253-267.

Pranggono, B., & Arabo, A. (2021). COVID-19 pandemic cybersecurity issues. *Internet Technology Letters*, 4(2), e247.

Quiroz-Gutierrez, M. (2022) The crown prince of Dubai says he has a 'metaverse strategy' that will add 40,000 jobs and $4 billions to the economy in 5 years. *Fortune*. Accessed on 20-July-2022. Available at https://fortune.com/2022/07/19/dubai-metaverse-strategy-crypto-emerging-tech-web3/

Randall, R. G., & Allen, S. (2021). Cybersecurity professionals information sharing sources and networks in the US electrical power industry. *International Journal of Critical Infrastructure Protection*, 100454.

Rashid, Z., Noor, U., & Altmann, J. (2021). Economic model for evaluating the value creation through information sharing within the cybersecurity information sharing ecosystem. *Future Generation Computer Systems*. 40

Richardson, R., North, M. M., & Garofalo, D. (2021). Ransomware: The landscape is shifting-a concise report. *International Management Review*, 17(1), 5-86.

Samson, M. (2022). Women and Girls in Science and Technology-2022 edition. Retrieved from Tang, C. S. (2022). Innovative technology and operations for alleviating poverty through women's economic empowerment. *Production and Operations Management*, 31(1), 32-45.

Sarkar, K. R. (2010). Assessing insider threats to information security using technical, behavioural and organisational measures. *Information security technical report*, 15(3), 112-133.

Schlienger, T., & Teufel, S. (2002). Information security culture. In: Ghonaimy, M.A., El-Hadidi, M.T., Aslan, H.K. (eds) *Security in the Information Society*. IFIP Advances in Information and Communication Technology, vol 86. Springer, Boston, MA. https://doi.org/10.1007/978-0-387-35586-3_16.

Schwab, K. (2017). *The fourth industrial revolution*. New York: Currency Books.

Scott, B., Mason, R., & Szewczyk, P. (2021). A snapshot analysis of publicly available BYOD policies. Paper presented at the *2021 Australasian Computer Science Week Multiconference*.

Serumaga-Zake, J. M., & van der Poll, J. A. (2021). Addressing the Impact of Fourth Industrial Revolution on South African Manufacturing Small and Medium Enterprises (SMEs). *Sustainability*, 13(21), 11703.

Sibert, W. O., & Baldwin, R. W. (2007). The Multics encipher_Algorithm. *Cryptologia*, 31(4), 292-304.

Singh, R. K., Luthra, S., Mangla, S. K., & Uniyal, S. (2019). Applications of information and communication technology for sustainable growth of SMEs in India food industry. *Resources, Conservation and Recycling*, 147, 10-18.

Smith, B. A., & Curran, K. (2021). Security Vulnerabilities in Microprocessors. *Semiconductor Science and Information Devices*, 3(1).

Snyder, T., & Byrd, G. (2017). The internet of everything. *Computer*, 50(06), 8-9.

Sommer, L. (2015). Industrial revolution-industry 4.0: Are German manufacturing SMEs the first victims of this revolution? *Journal of Industrial Engineering and Management*, 8(5), 1512-1532.

Spafford, E. (1989). Crisis and aftermath (the Internet worm). *Comm. of the ACM*, 32(6), 678-687.

Straub, D. W. (1990). Effective IS security: An empirical study. *Information systems research*, 1(3), 255-276.

Straub, D. W., & Welke, R. J. (1998). Coping with systems risk: Security planning models for management decision making. *MIS quarterly*, 441-469.

Thompson, D. (2015). The Secret to Smart Groups: It's Women. *The Atlantic*. Retrieved from https://www.theatlantic.com/business/archive/2015/01/the-secretto-smart-groups-isnt-smart-people/384625/.

Triana, M. d. C., Miller, T. L., & Trzebiatowski, T. M. (2014). The double-edged nature of board gender diversity: Diversity, firm performance, and the power of women directors as predictors of strategic change. *Organization Science*, 25(2), 609-632.

Vance, A., Lowry, P. B., & Eggett, D. (2015). Increasing Accountability Through User-Interface Design Artifacts. *MIS quarterly*, 39(2), 345- 366.

Van Haastrecht, M., Sarhan, I., Shojaifar, A., Baumgartner, L., Mallouli, W., & Spruit, M. (2021). A Threat-Based Cybersecurity Risk Assessment Approach Addressing SME Needs. Paper presented at the *The 16th International Conference on Availability, Reliability and Security*.

Van Niekerk, J., & Von Solms, R. (2010). Information security culture: A management perspective. *Computers & security*, 29(4), 476-486.

Verbeek, P.-P. (2005). *What things do: Philosophical reflections on technology, agency, and design.* Transated by Robert P. Crease. University Park, PA: Pennsylvania State University Press.

Vimalkumar, M., Singh, J. B., & Gouda, S. K. (2021). Contextualizing the relationship between Gender and Computer Self-efficacy: An Empirical study from India. *Information & Management*, 58(4), 103464.

Vooren, M., Haelermans, C., Groot, W., & van den Brink, H. M. (2022). Comparing success of female students to their male counterparts in the STEM fields: an empirical analysis from enrollment until graduation using longitudinal register data. *International Journal of STEM Education*, 9(1), 1-17.

Wellalage, N., & Locke, S. (2017). Access to credit by SMEs in South Asia: do women entrepreneurs face discrimination. *Research in International Business and Finance*, 41, 336-346.

Weston, G. (2022). 5 Profitable Business Opportunities In Metaverse. *101 Blockchains*, Accessed on 20-July-2022. Available at https://101blockchains.com/business-opportunities-in-metaverse/.

Wibowo, R. M., & Sulaksono, A. (2021). Web Vulnerability Through Cross Site Scripting (XSS) Detection with OWASP Security Shepherd. *Indonesian Journal of Information Systems,* 3(2), 149-159.

Zhou, Z., Gaurav, A., Gupta, B., Hamdi, H., & Nedjah, N. (2021). A statistical approach to secure health care services from DDoS attacks during COVID-19 pandemic. *Neural Computing and Applications*, 1-14.

Index

#

4IR technologies, vii, 6, 7, 9, 29, 35, 59, 75, 82, 83, 86, 88

A

artificial intelligence, viii, 1, 6, 9, 42, 75, 76, 82

B

big data, viii, 6, 35, 75, 77, 78, 79, 80, 81, 82, 83, 86, 89, 91, 94, 97
bottom-up approach, 13

C

CIA triad, 5, 7
code-breakers, 4
collaborative tools, 64, 66, 88
Computer Security Institute, 18
coronavirus, 3, 32, 63
COVID-19, viii, 3, 14, 32, 33, 35, 55, 59, 60, 61, 62, 63, 64, 65, 66, 86, 87, 93, 94, 95, 96, 97, 100
cybercrimes, 13, 34
cybersecurity, vii, viii, 1, 2, 3, 4, 6, 7, 9, 10, 12, 13, 19, 20, 21, 22, 23, 24, 25, 26, 27, 28, 29, 30, 31, 32, 33, 34, 35, 37, 38, 39, 40, 41, 43, 45, 48, 49, 50, 51, 52, 53, 54, 55, 56, 57, 58, 59, 66, 68, 76, 77, 85, 86, 87, 88, 89, 93, 94, 95, 96, 97, 98, 99
cybersecurity risks, vii, viii, 7, 9, 13, 23, 24, 29, 35

cybersecurity threats, vii, viii, 1, 2, 3, 7, 13, 22, 23, 24, 25, 28, 29, 30, 34, 37, 39, 56, 57, 59, 66, 85, 86, 87
cyberterrorism, 16
cyberwarfare, 13

D

decision-support systems (DSS), 11

E

email, 30, 33, 60
executive support systems (ESS), 11, 12

F

fifth-generation (5G), 30, 31, 35, 86
fourth industrial revolution (4IR), vii, viii, 1, 2, 6, 7, 9, 18, 29, 35, 59, 75, 76, 80, 82, 83, 86, 88, 98
fourth-generation (4G), 30, 31

G

GDP, 6, 54

H

hackers, 3, 14, 15, 19, 22, 32, 72, 85
hacktivism, 13

I

information security, vii, viii, ix, 3, 5, 7, 12, 13, 14, 15, 17, 18, 19, 20, 22, 28, 37, 38, 39, 40, 41, 42, 43, 45, 48, 49, 51, 53, 54, 55, 56, 58, 62, 63, 66, 72, 73, 75, 76, 77, 78, 81, 82, 85, 86, 87, 88, 89, 93, 94, 95, 96, 97, 98
information security risk management, vii
Internet of Everything, 82, 97, 99
Internet of Things (IoT), 6, 18, 31, 35, 42, 52, 57, 71, 75, 82, 83, 86, 91, 95, 97

L

lockdowns, viii, 3, 33, 55, 59, 60, 64, 86

M

machine learning, viii, 35, 76, 77, 82, 83, 86, 89, 95
malware, 2, 3, 9, 15, 16, 19, 23, 33, 34, 56, 60, 63, 65, 76, 77
management information system (MIS), 11, 94, 99
man-in-the-middle attack, 4
Metaverse, viii, 67, 69, 70, 71, 72, 73, 88, 98, 99

N

National Institute of Standards and Technology (NIST), 25, 26, 32, 98
National Small Business Association, 59

P

phishing, 2, 3, 16, 27, 33, 56, 57, 60, 61, 64, 72

R

ransomware, 16, 27, 63, 66, 77, 88, 96, 98

S

security controls, 61
security threat, vii, viii, ix, 14, 17, 25, 27, 33, 39, 43, 51, 62, 66, 72, 79, 80, 87
software attacks, 16
South African Department of Trade and Industry, 2
STEM, 45, 46, 49, 52, 53, 95, 99

T

top-down approach, 13
transaction processing system (TPS), 10, 11, 98, 99

U

United States Department of Health and Human Services, 61

W

women entrepreneurs, viii, 45, 46, 47, 54, 55, 57, 58, 87, 99